AN
INVITATION
TO
hea ing

AN
INVITATION
TO
healing

Let God Touch Your
Mind, Body and Spirit

Lynda D. Elliott

Chosen Books

A Division of Baker Book House Co
Grand Rapids, Michigan 49516

Published by Chosen Books
A division of Baker Book House Company
P.O. Box 6287, Grand Rapids, MI 49516-6287

Printed in the United States of America

Library of Congress Cataloging-in-Publication Data

Elliott, Lynda D.
    An invitation to healing / Lynda D. Elliot.
        p.   cm.
    ISBN 0-8007-9286-6
      1. Healing—Religious aspects—Christianity. 2. Suffering—Religious
aspects—Christianity. I. Title.
BT732.E455 2001
234′.131—dc21   2001017490

Scripture is taken from the Amplified New Testament. Copyright © 1954, 1958,
1987 by the Lockman Foundation; and the Amplified Bible, Old Testament. Copyright © 1965, 1987 by The Zondervan Corporation. Used by permission.

Scripture marked NIV is taken from the HOLY BIBLE, NEW INTERNATIONAL
VERSION®. NIV®. Copyright © 1973, 1978, 1984, by International Bible Soci-
ety. Used by permission of Zondervan Publishing House. All rights reserved.

To protect the privacy of some of the individuals referred to, names, places and
other details have been changed.

For current information about all releases from Baker Book House, visit our web site:
http://www.bakerbooks.com

Dedicated to

Wayne
my husband and best friend

CONTENTS

ACKNOWLEDGMENTS

I want to express special thanks to friends who have inspired me, prayed for me and constantly encouraged me in the writing of this book. You are treasures in my life! I appreciate you—Carolyn Johnson, Nancy Grisham, Jane Anne Smith, Joy White, Carolyn Russell, Nina Cameron, Barbara Benson, Carole Harvey, Pamela Peterson, Debbie Darby, Lynda Sorrells, Jananne Reding, Ellen Sambrano, Libby Strawn, Anne Loveless and a wonderful new treasure, Jan Silvious.

I want to express appreciation to my editors, Jane Campbell and Ann Weinheimer, who saw the value of this book. You are the experts! You are also so enjoyable, encouraging and fun.

The people who contributed their stories to me are invaluable. You have given me entrance into the pain and joy of your lives. Thank you for allowing me to know you and to record what God has done for you. May your lives be blessed in every way!

My appreciation would not be complete without expressing appreciation to Dr. Tom Fletcher and Dr. Larrian Gillespie. God used you to provide healing for me. Thank you!

Introduction

My search for healing began 35 years ago as I watched my father slowly die, one painful, agonizing moment at a time. As several illnesses consumed his body, his mind began to bear the burden of the merciless assault; he often lost consciousness or became delusional. Near the end of his life his physical being consisted mostly of skin, bones and a few oozing bed sores. He would look at me with glazed eyes and ask, "Who are you and where did you come from?" I was nineteen years old and I had no idea what to say, think or do. I was terribly afraid.

As I sat by his bed doubt began to enter my mind for the first time. How could God let the life of one of His faithful servants end this way? Did He not see the loss of personal human dignity? Did He not care? If He cared, how could He bear the sorrow of my father's pitiful condition? Did it not matter because all would be well on "the other side" of life? What about this side of life? Was this the best God had to offer those who were suffering?

My father finally died, having forgotten who he was or who anyone else was. I wondered if he remembered who God was and if he still had faith in Him. I was almost completely overwhelmed by feelings of absolute helplessness and disbelief. As I looked at his wasted body I could find no resemblance to the short, stocky man with the twinkling eyes who had been a deacon in our church—the one who, with just a wink, sent my girlfriends and me into giggles of delight when he passed the offering plate down our pew. How could God let such a horrible thing happen to such a good man?

Grief-stricken and confused I sat at his funeral—which was my first—and thought, *What a terrible ending to a life that has been lived with Christian dignity, integrity and kindness!* Somehow, I lost a little of my childhood trust in God at that moment, but at the same time the Holy Spirit stirred within me a desire to know more about God's healing power. I wanted to know if such suffering could be avoided. That desire stayed with me through the slow death of my husband's parents as they both died of cancer a few months apart, and it increased as I became responsible for the care of my mother, who suffered the darkness of clinical depression for six years. Whereas my father's body had been assaulted by disease, my mother's mind was defeated by bitterness, hopelessness and fear.

I walked the breeding ground of questions regarding healing, witnessing the need for God's healing hand to be placed upon those who suffered. *Surely God wants more than this for His children!* I thought, and as years passed I found that He definitely did! The first evidence came through my mother's miracle, which I will describe for you later in this book.

Am I saying that my father and my husband's parents did not have to suffer and die the way they did? As I look back I can see clearly that our knowledge and experience were very limited. Isaiah 55:11 says: "So shall My word be that goes forth out of My mouth; it shall not return to Me void—without producing any effect, useless—but it shall accomplish that which I please and purpose, and it shall prosper in the thing for which I sent it." Because God's Word always makes a difference, I believe that their lives and deaths would have been different if we had known then what we know now.

Would they have been healed? This raises the question that is always present when healing is discussed: Why isn't everyone healed? I want to tell you now that I cannot give you the answer to that question. I am sure that you, as well as I, can tell many stories of those who suffered and died as my father did. I can, however, present what God has taught me from His Word and confirmed through healing in my life and in the lives of many others.

God's healing ways. . . . They are many. They are varied. If you or someone you love needs physical, emotional or spiritual healing, my prayer is that this book will be a catalyst for your personal search. Psalm 16:11 says: "You will show me the path of life; in Your presence is fullness of joy, at Your right hand there are pleasures for evermore." As we journey together may you become more deeply acquainted with Him and experience true spiritual joy.

PRELUDE TO HEALING

Do you know the difference between simply receiving knowledge from information via your intellect and receiving direct revelation from the Holy Spirit? If you do, you know that at certain moments in your life a "light" will come on in your mind enabling you to see more than usual. You suddenly have insight and clarity beyond what your normal faculties can offer. The stimulus for the revelation may be the Word of God, a "word of knowledge" from another person, response to a prayer, surfacing of memories or simply the still, small Voice speaking to you. But the Holy Spirit is there working in you.

As I share my story with you, ask the Holy Spirit to work within you personally. Listen for the revelations He will give you. Although God has many mysteries, He promises to give us truth. Deuteronomy 29:29 tells us: "The secret things belong unto the Lord our God; but the things which are revealed belong to us and to our children for ever, that we may do all of the words of this law." Just because you may have unanswered questions, do not be discouraged in your search for healing. Do not allow someone else's experience to be the baseline for your knowledge and faith. Listen for Him to speak to you. John 14:26 tells us that the Holy Spirit is our Comforter, Counselor, Helper and Advocate, and that He will teach us all things. Rely on Him. Get quiet and listen.

Concerning those who have not been healed, do not blame God and do not blame yourself. Suffering is difficult enough without the heavy burden of judgment. In the first chapter we will look at some of the known blocks to healing. Perhaps God will reveal a block to your or someone else's healing. Move from the past into your present search and let yourself be taught and led by the power of the Holy Spirit.

God's Ways Are Many and Varied

During my years as a social worker I have spent many hours listening to those who suffer all types of afflictions. I have found that God works in a variety of ways to help His children. My friend Kelly, for instance, experienced two varied healing adventures. One came in the form of a miracle—an instantaneous intervention from God—and the other was progressive, requiring her participation.

In 1980 when Kelly was working temporarily out of state, she was invited to a picnic at a park several miles from town. She was driving her rental car along unfamiliar winding roads at dusk when an oncoming speeding car forced her off the road. Her car plunged down a deep ravine and hit a tree, throwing her through the windshield and then back into the car. Kelly suffered many injuries. The bones in her face were crushed and her teeth were knocked out. Her right ankle was almost completely severed. Barely conscious, but remembering her ten-year-old daughter, Kelly forced herself to climb out of the car, holding onto her ankle. She was pulling herself up the ravine when help finally arrived.

For weeks Kelly wrestled between life and death. Her husband, overwhelmed by her condition, abandoned her. I wanted to write to Kelly, offering her hope in God's healing power, but like her husband I was also overwhelmed by her condition. I did not have the faith to give her that assurance. Instead I wrote a letter telling her that I was asking Jesus Christ to come to her room and visit her. I learned several weeks later that my letter had been misplaced at the hospital and had not yet arrived on the night when Kelly reached the point of death. On that night, as Kelly lay there in pain, she saw beams of light pouring into her room. She experienced the presence of Jesus Christ. He gave her the hope that I did not have the faith to give. Several days later she received my lost letter, telling her that I was asking Jesus to come and help her. That confirmation bolstered her faith and she became committed to the healing process.

From that time on Kelly's condition began to improve. Her face was restored through plastic surgery, her teeth were replaced, her bones began to mend and her ankle started to heal. After months of surgery and physical therapy, she was able to return to work.

Considering the severity of the injury to her ankle, doctors were amazed that they did not have to amputate her right foot. Not only did Kelly get to keep her foot, she was finally able to lay aside her cane and in time she was jogging! The whole experience was spiritually and emotionally life-changing, bringing her closer to God and developing a new depth of character.

What would have happened to Kelly after the accident if she had let herself become lost in pain and despair? What if she had not been completely committed to the healing process? Could she have made such an astounding recovery? I do not think so.

This healing is an example of God's progressive healing power, plus the determination and obedience of someone who desperately desired to be well. Much was required of Kelly, but God met her at every point of the healing process.

Years later Kelly faced another life-threatening situation and this time received God's immediate intervention. Because of a minor heart condition, she was directed to take an antibiotic immediately following a dental appointment. As she left the dental office, she hurriedly crammed the prescription into her pocket and forgot about it. Several days later Kelly became very sick. The cause of her illness remained a mystery for weeks and, once again, Kelly's life was in danger.

When she finally connected her illness to the forgotten prescription, the alarm heightened: Doctors discovered a clump of infection attached to the wall of her heart. Open-heart surgery was scheduled immediately. If the clump broke loose it would travel directly to her brain or lungs, bringing instant death.

Several friends gathered around her bed the night before her surgery and observed the clump of infection on a video screen in her room. We held our breath as every heartbeat seemed to cause it to shudder, threatening to loosen it. At her request we prayed one more time for healing.

The next morning after surgery the doctor approached us, clearly mystified. He told us that the clump of infection had simply disappeared. He had not been able to find it! God had intervened again for Kelly's life.

In this instance there was nothing Kelly could offer in the way of discipline or obedience. She was helpless and God undertook her healing process. God fulfills His purposes through a variety of healing methods, blessing His children in the ways of His choice.

Our Part in the Journey

Once a middle-aged woman named Jane, having suffered for years with depression and severe headaches, said this to me: "I guess I thought that when I pray, healing should come almost like a kind of magic. In fact, it never occurred to me that I would need to do more than pray, take medicine and hope for the best. I had absolutely no idea that my attitudes or behavior could prolong my condition!"

Jane had been a believer in Christ for more than ten years when she had an affair with a man who worked in her office. Knowing that adultery was wrong, she discontinued the relationship and asked God to forgive her. Regardless of her repentance, however, depression continued to overshadow her, affecting all areas of her life.

After we visited together several times, Jane told me that the most humiliating night of her life came when she had finally gained the courage to tell her lover that she would no longer be available for him. To her surprise he had simply shrugged and replied, "I don't really mind letting you go. You're not all I thought you'd be." The affair had cost Jane everything—her marriage, her home, her comfortable lifestyle and her job. She was extremely angry. Her lover left with no expression of sorrow, which convinced her that she had indeed meant nothing to him. When her husband insisted upon getting a divorce, she grew angry with him as well because he no longer wanted her either.

Day after day, as Jane counted her losses, her anger gained momentum. It drained all of her emotional and physical energy and drove her deeper and deeper into depression. Her headaches became debilitating. Because of her shame, Jane would not allow herself to speak of her affair to anyone, carefully burying her anger inside.

Then, when she learned that the weight of her buried anger was the root of her depression, she became more than willing to let God lead her through a process of restoration. Although her recovery was not magic, it was miraculous. She humbled herself, faced the block of bitterness inside and released her anger. As she forgave herself and others, God washed the anger away. Soon after, her depression lifted and her headaches ceased.

Many of us are like Jane. We have some form of *disease,* but we attribute it to some malfunction of our minds or bodies, as though we had almost nothing to do with it. We do not realize that the body and mind are hooked up to work together, and it is the spirit that is meant to be the cornerstone of both.

This book is the story of my search for healing. In it we will look at personal experiences and many healing stories, along with what I have found in God's Word. It is divided into four sections: the area of hidden blocks to healing; the need to discern God's will; finding the power to endure possible hardship; and discovering avenues we can take toward the healing God desires for us.

In Exodus 15:26 God introduces Himself to us by saying, "I am the Lord Who heals you." As we begin our journey, ask God to reveal Himself as your Healer. He is waiting for you to discover the fullness of His compassion.

Blocks to Healing

The spirit of man . . . is the lamp of the Lord, searching all his innermost parts.

Proverbs 20:27

Is it possible to block God's healing touch? Can we override His plan to make us well? The answer is yes, and unless we are willing to face those blocks—painful though it might be—and let God cleanse us from their effects, we will not move toward the healing we desire. As you look at the blocks to healing that are explained in this chapter, ask the Holy Spirit to search your heart, revealing spiritual, emotional and physical truth to you. Listen carefully.

21

Guilt and Unacknowledged, Unconfessed Sin

Dr. Paul Tournier, Swiss psychiatrist and Christian, once said, "A bad conscience can, over a period of years, so strangle a person's life that his physical and mental powers of resistance to disease are thereby impaired. It can be the root cause of certain psychosomatic afflictions. It is like a stopper which must be pulled out by confession so that life may begin to flow again."

Conviction of sin is one of the responsibilities of the Holy Spirit. He wants us to acknowledge and confess the sin so that His healing power will not be blocked from flowing into our lives. If we ignore His gentle prodding and choose not to confess our sins, we are going to bear the penalty of guilt, believing that we are not worthy of God's healing. For example, a young woman named Sally who had contracted a sexually transmitted disease told me this: "How could I believe that God would heal me from this? I got it while I was committing adultery! Really, I don't deserve to get well." As Sally sat before me expressing her feelings of worthlessness, tears streaming down her face, I felt God's compassion for her. She was caught in the trap of self-condemnation. Because Sally felt unworthy, she condemned herself to her illness. She did not understand that our Father wanted to forgive her and restore her health, as well as her life. Because of her hopelessness and despair, Sally had even neglected to take the prescribed medication. *In her guilt and error, she had sabotaged her own healing.*

Are you sabotaging your healing in some way because you feel unworthy? Is a block of guilt in your way? Is it causing you unnecessary harm?

The Redeeming Qualities of Guilt

The destructive effects of guilt were obvious in Sally's life; however, this does not have to be the outcome. If we understand the redemptive purposes of guilt and respond accordingly, guilt *can* lead us to health and well-being. God reveals His motives for allowing guilt in our lives in 2 Corinthians 7:10 where He tells us that "godly grief and the pain God is permitted to direct, produce a repentance that leads and contributes to salvation and deliverance from evil, and it never brings regret."

In fact, the purpose of guilt is similar to that of a smoke alarm. A smoke alarm sends a signal that something is going wrong inside the house and gives us the chance to escape. When we begin to experience the conviction of sin (guilt) and respond correctly to our internal alarm system, we then have the privilege of making new choices and changing our direction . . . avoiding pain and potential destruction.

The Effects of Prolonged Guilt

In Psalm 31:10 we read about the emotional and physical torment King David experienced following his sin and before he received forgiveness. He says: "For my life is spent with sorrow, and my years with sighing; my strength has failed me because of my iniquity; even my bones have wasted away."

David continues: "There is no soundness in my flesh . . . neither is there any health or rest in my bones because of my sin. For my iniquities are gone over my head [like waves of a flood]: as a heavy burden they weigh too much for me. My wounds are loathsome and corrupt because of my foolishness. I am bent and bowed down greatly; I go about mourning all the day long. . . . My heart throbs, my strength fails me. . . . For I do confess my guilt and iniquity; I am filled with sorrow for my sin. . . . Make haste to help me, O Lord" (Psalm 38:3–6, 10, 18, 22).

Finally David finds relief: "For day and night Your hand [of displeasure] was heavy upon me. . . . I acknowledged my sin to You, and my iniquity I did not hide. I said, I will confess my transgressions to the Lord [continually unfolding the past till all is told], then You [instantly] forgave me the guilt and iniquity of my sin" (Psalm 32:4–5).

Have you ever felt the depth of despair that King David did? Are you ready to be restored from the effects of your sin? If you are, let guilt do its desired work and bring you to the point of confession of your sin. Do not allow guilt to continue to harm you. *Let it rescue you!*

Confession of Sin

As the Holy Spirit convicts us of sin and we acknowledge its existence, we turn to James 5:13–16 to learn our next step. Here we see the need to confess our sins to one another. Confession, whether another person is present or not, is invaluable when sin has promoted a prolonged, deep sense of guilt or caused self-destructive behavior. I have confessed every sin that has had a significant impact on my conscience and life to someone I trust. Sometimes we need assurance from another human being, as well as from God, that we are still lovable and acceptable. Then, regardless of our sin, we can begin to *feel* the release that we have already been freely given.

As Sally anguished over her illness and sin, she uncovered the lie that bound her to her illness—*the need for continued punishment.* She exclaimed, "I think God wants me to feel this pain the rest of my life, so that I'll remember never to commit adultery again!"

Sally did not understand the depths of God's mercy and provision for her. Although it may be possible for the consequences of past sin to influence us toward righteousness in the future, we do not have to oppress ourselves with painful memories in order not to sin again. Instead, as we let Him, the Holy Spirit will guide us and keep us free. Romans 6:14 tells us: "For sin shall not [any longer] exert dominion over you, since now you are not under Law [as slaves], but under grace—as subjects of God's favor and mercy."

As Sally expressed her fears and then heard God's Word regarding guilt and confession, her relief became evident. She finally realized that God simply wanted her to have a heart of obedience toward Him. She understood that God does not condone sin, but neither does He get satisfaction from punishing us with constant reminders of what we did wrong or from watching us continue to punish ourselves.

If you have been bearing the pain of guilt or deliberately punishing yourself, would you like for that to stop? You are the only one who can stop it. Are you ready? If you are, do as James 5 instructs. Confess your sin to God as well as to another person if necessary. Then you will have no valid reason to continue experiencing the guilt that could cause you to sabotage your healing.

Recognizing and Rejecting False Guilt

Do you know what false guilt is? False guilt is the feeling that comes when we take the blame or responsibility for what someone else did. It causes the same emotional and physiological damage as real guilt. I worked with an incest survivor who expressed her feelings this way: "My father told me the sexual abuse was my fault . . . that I was a prissy little girl who flaunted herself before him. He told me that he wouldn't have had the desire to abuse me if I had not sat in his lap or crawled into his bed at night. I've felt guilty since I was a little girl. I believe I caused the incest."

This is a clear example of false guilt. Sexual perpetrators almost always blame their victims for their crimes. When the abuse is perpetrated against small children who do not know better, false guilt takes deep roots and contaminates their self-image. They absorb the guilt for a crime that is not theirs and often remain victims.

Not every instance of false guilt is as easy to determine as this one. How can you tell the difference between real guilt and false guilt? A survivor of sexual abuse once gave me an excellent definition: "I see now that valid guilt comes from the convicting power of the Holy Spirit, and there is no condemnation in it. Valid guilt signals an invitation to righteousness. In contrast, false guilt is accompanied by false accusations, manipulation, condemnation, fear and bondage."

I was counseling a woman named Marianne who had so much false guilt heaped upon her that she felt responsible for every bad thing that happened around her. Even her body language communicated her emotional burden as she sat before me slumped in her chair, her arms folded over her chest. To help bring light into her situation, I told her of reading about an earthquake in Japan and described the tragic losses. She immediately sat straight up and exclaimed, "How terrible! I'm so sorry!" With a smile, I responded, "Now, what do you think you might have done to cause that?" Because Marianne had lived with so much false guilt, she actually began for a moment to grasp mentally for ways in which she could have initiated that disaster!

Would you like to stop penalizing yourself for something that you did not do? If you would, ask the Holy Spirit to bring clarity to your mind. If you have been bound to the effects of false guilt, let yourself be released. Do it now.

The Effects of Shame

Another deadly block to healing is a sense of shame. Shame comes when we have not sought forgiveness and our actions are exposed. Some of us wear shame like a second skin. It is not unusual to hear someone describe himself as shame-based, meaning that his relationship with God as well as with others is based on shame.

Shame is like a vacuum cleaner, sucking up life wherever it goes. Shame also has several "attachments" . . . fear of exposure, fear of rejection and loss of present and future opportunities. Shame keeps us from healing because it promotes a feeling of unworthiness similar to that of guilt. It also exists in true and false forms.

Authentic Shame

When we are living against the will of God and our sin is exposed, we feel legitimate shame. Like true guilt, legitimate shame is another part of the internal warning system. When we experience this alarming feeling, we can choose to seek God's forgiveness and change direction. Then we can be released from the need for shame, as well as the risk of exposure.

Isaiah reminds us of God's generosity and compassion toward those who have repented of sin: "For your [former] shame you shall have a twofold recompense; instead of dishonor and reproach your people shall rejoice in their portion; . . . they shall possess double [what they had forfeited]; everlasting joy shall be theirs" (Isaiah 61:7).

False Shame

False shame comes when we internalize what someone has said about us and call it truth. When we do this, we are no longer looking at sin and repentance. Instead we are making deceiving decisions about ourselves.

For example, an attractive, intelligent woman named Clarice fell into this trap. "I've felt ashamed ever since my husband left me for a woman he met at the gym," she said. "On the last day, as he packed his suitcase, he said that I had been a terrible wife and that it was my fault he had had an affair! I've just become emotionally paralyzed. I don't feel as though anyone would want to know me. I've been too ashamed to make new friends, much less consider going out on a date."

Clarice had internalized her husband's remarks as truth about herself, condemning herself to the shameful image that he had projected upon her. The truth is that her husband should be bearing the shame because of his decision to be unfaithful and abandon her. Instead he maliciously chose to project his shame onto her and she accepted it.

If you have absorbed a sense of shame due to someone's opinion of you or actions toward you, ask the Holy Spirit to show you how much God loves and delights in you. If your sins are forgiven, there is no need to bear shame or declare yourself unworthy to receive God's blessings. Do not allow yourself to continue to be in the bondage of shame to the words or actions of another human being. Release yourself to receive healing.

Shame and Self-Condemnation

Can you see that someone who feels shame also holds the remnants of a judgmental, condemning perspective? This is because our fear of exposure leads to anticipating negative behavior in others. For example, we may think: *If they knew this, they would never trust me again!* or *If they knew this about me, they would never respect me. In fact, they would abandon me.* When we allow these thoughts to go unchecked we are *judging* others before they have had a chance to respond.

A vivacious, petite woman named Joy told me her story. "I want to testify that it is possible to be 'free' but enslaved," she said. "As I led Bible studies, led a church ministry and shared the Gospel I would say to myself, 'There is therefore now no condemnation for those who are in Christ Jesus.' The problem was that I didn't believe it for myself.

"Many years ago I committed a sin for which I couldn't forgive myself or receive the forgiveness of God, even though I asked over and over to be forgiven. Whenever someone expressed gratitude to me or complimented me in any way I would think, *If only you knew what I did, you wouldn't feel that way.*

"I began to learn about letting go of guilt, shame and fear. My Bible study teacher said, 'Imagine that you have a twelve-year-old daughter who is getting dressed for her first party. She is so excited, turning before the mirror, exclaiming that she looks beautiful in her new dress. Now imagine that as she walks out of the house, you catch her and say, "Have a wonderful time at the party, but remember how you cheated in the third grade!"' I sat there stunned and I thought to myself, *I would never do that!* At that moment the Holy Spirit spoke to me and showed me that I was saying similar things to myself every day!"

Joy's transformation began with the revelation from God that she had shamed herself in a way that she would not treat her own child. Her revelation was immediately followed by an opportunity for deliverance from shame.

Joy continued: "I was ready for the next step. I was ready to comply with the directions in the book of James about confession, so I called a good friend and asked for a meeting. I went to her house with great fear, not knowing what she would say. But after I confessed my sin to her, she anointed me with oil and prayed for me to be completely delivered and healed . . . and I was. There was no condemnation from her, nor was there any from my Father.

"I had wanted to love God passionately for years, but my self-imposed bondage had blocked my acceptance of His love as well as my love for Him. Now that all condemnation and shame are gone, I can feel His love. I can enjoy the party!"

Can you see the judgmental basis in shame? Judgment of self and others? It is true that some people might reject us if they really knew all about us, but God will strengthen us to deal with such responses if they do indeed ever come about. The most evil bondage is to live "as if" the worst has already occurred.

Forgetting What Lies Behind . . .

Fear is not the only reason that we might not let go of shame. Sometimes we hold onto the memories of our sins because we believe that it is noble to do so. We think: *Considering what I did, it doesn't seem fair for me to forget it and go on!* However, if we have been forgiven and cleansed, it is not noble to recall our sins. Neither is it helpful, nor does it reflect the deep mercies of God. We must join with Paul who says, "Forgetting what lies behind and straining forward to what lies ahead, I press on toward the goal . . ." (Philippians 3:13–14).

We cannot move into the future as long as we insist on remaining attached to the past. That would be like attempting to ice skate with one skate pointing forward and the other one backward. Our minds and thinking will remain "split." As James 1:6–8 says, "Only it must be in faith that he asks, with no wavering—no hesitating, no doubting. . . . For truly, let not such a person imagine that he will receive anything [he asks for] from the Lord, [for being as he is] a man of two minds—hesitating, dubious, irresolute—[he is] unstable and unreliable and uncertain about everything (he thinks, feels, decides)."

Can We Really Forget Our Shame?

Just as Paul "forgets" what lies behind, Isaiah 54:4 promises us that it is possible to forget the shame of our past. God assures us that it is not His desire for His children to bear shame. Nothing can be gained by it. Although we cannot totally erase the *memories,* we can decide to allow God to remove the *effects* of those memories. We can cease to be affected or controlled by them. Yes, there may be some consequences of sin that we must bear, but we no longer have to carry the guilt or shame. We are commanded *to forget* (lay aside, cease to call attention to), so let's accept our freedom and begin to heal.

Are you ready to give up your shame? To stop waiting for the "other shoe" of exposure to fall? Are you like Joy—ready to move forward? Remember that this is your decision. Keep in mind that it will directly affect your well-being for the rest of your life. Are you ready to trust God with your past? If you are, seek forgiveness, make any restitution that may be required and lay the past aside.

Psalm 124:7 says that "we are like a bird escaped from the snare of the fowlers; the snare is broken, and we have escaped!" Your way of escape lies before you. All you have to do is begin walking forward.

Disobedience

Once I met a man who had refused for years to stop smoking, and when he found that he had cancer in one lung, he still refused to quit. He decided that he would rather die smoking than live without cigarettes. So, his choice was made.

As his condition worsened, however, he asked, "Why is God doing this to me?" *The truth is that he did it to himself!* And he is not alone. We have many ways to make ourselves sick via the food we eat, lack of exercise, overwork, alcohol, drugs, sexual addictions . . . the avenues are endless and we should not blame God for our poor choices.

On the other hand, a fifty-year-old, gray-haired man named Tom had suffered physically and emotionally for years and was willing to make any changes in his lifestyle. He prayed constantly but experienced no relief. Finally he began attending a support group at his church. Following the first meeting he said, "I was just amazed! Over and over I heard the same type of statement from the group members: 'When I obeyed the Word of God I began to feel better' or 'When I forgave my mother/father I began to have relief.' Another one said, 'When I gave up my anger at Dad, my stomach pain stopped.' As these men began to learn what God required and began to obey, they began to experience healing."

Tom continued: "It was a relief to know what God wanted from me. I had no idea that I had been making myself sick. It helped to know that I could participate in my own healing. Knowing this causes the process to seem more concrete and less elusive."

Is it not interesting how one man saw obedience as a stumbling block and another man saw obedience as an opportunity? Obedience may be difficult at times, but it is a small price to pay for the healing of emotional, spiritual or physical pain.

Has God shown you any areas of disobedience in your life? Are you ready to forgive someone who has greatly harmed you? Are you willing to make restitution, if required, for harm that you have done to someone? Are you ready to give up a harmful habit? How do you perceive this opportunity to obey God?

Two illustrations from Scripture show that obedience may be required for healing. The first is John 9:10–11, which says: "So they said to him, How were your eyes opened? He replied, The Man called Jesus made mud and smeared it on my eyes and said to me, Go to Siloam and wash. *So I went and washed,* and I obtained my sight!" (emphasis added). The second is Mark 2:9–12 in which a man was healed *as he picked up his bed and walked.* If he had not attempted to walk, how could he possibly have known he was healed? Through his obedience, he found his healing. Other instructions are in James 5:15–20, as I mentioned earlier.

I once heard a pastor ask a wise question, "Do you want to be healed? If so, how much? Are you willing to do whatever it takes?" Continuing to probe, he asked, "Are you willing to give up your pride?"

Can you recall a time when you took a deep breath and began to speak the words that allowed the stronghold of pride in your life to come down? Sometimes the simple statement "I was wrong. Will you forgive me?"

is the beginning of healing, both emotionally as well as physically. Those words have great impact in the spiritual realm.

Are you ready to decide what you want? How much do you want it? Are you willing to do absolutely anything it takes? If you are, take the first step of obedience now.

Fear of Recovery

Have you ever seen someone refuse every avenue of help that is offered? I knew a woman once who had this attitude: "I've been sick and off work for so long that I don't think I could get a job if I got well. Besides, being on disability has become a convenience for me and I've allowed my work skills to become stagnant. I really think I would rather bear my illness than recover and have to go back to 'real life' and find a job." That woman had decided in favor of her illness, and there was no way that she would give it up!

Think of the man at the pool of Bethesda (see John 5:2–9). He had been there for 38 years. Imagine what a change healing would make in his life. He probably would have to get a job and become a contributing, responsible person in the work force again. He had to decide to give up all of the perceived benefits of his illness before he could receive his healing. Obviously, he was willing to do so.

It is wise to ask ourselves, *What would change about my life if I got well? Would I truly welcome those changes?* In some ways, healing is definitely a matter of choice. Have you chosen? Do you see yourself in the descriptions that follow?

The Need for Attention

A frail woman named Emma told me the following: "I'm almost afraid to get well. My entire life revolves around this condition. My daughter comes every Wednesday to take me to the grocery store, and I look forward to that. My pastor comes every Thursday to pray for me. My neighbor mows my lawn. They all ask about my condition. All of our conversations revolve around my illness. What would we talk about if I felt better? I'm afraid no one would come if I actually got well."

Emma was placing her faith in her illness, not realizing that God was her Provider or believing that she could trust Him with each day of her life. She was so focused on maintaining her attention-getting system that she had lost sight of the needs of those around her.

Have you ever noticed how many of us are identified by our illnesses or trials? For example,

"She is an arthritic."
"He is a polio survivor."
"She is the one who is so depressed."
"She is the woman whose child died last year."
"She is the one whose husband left her."
"He is the man who lost his fortune."

And we identify ourselves in the same manner:

"I am an incest survivor."
"I am an arthritic . . . an asthmatic . . . a paraplegic."

We must be careful that the flags flying over our heads do not carry the names of afflictions and that we are not "identified as" an illness or condition. We are human beings, God's children, and His Word tells us that His banner over us is love (see Song of Solomon 2:4). When we think of ourselves according to our illnesses or misfortunes, we limit our own perceptions of ourselves. We mentally enforce limits on our opportunities. And we train others to see us in the same way.

In order to become well, it is possible that Emma would need to trust God, forget herself and begin to serve others. At times when I have experienced sickness, grief or confusion, investing myself in others has been a relief. When I have done all I can do about my own circumstances, I feel better knowing that I can help someone else. Service truly can bring the blessing of relief.

Isaiah 58:6–8 illustrates the healing power that comes from thinking of others:

> Is not this the fast that I have chosen . . . ? Is it not to divide your bread with the hungry, and bring the homeless poor into your house? When you see the naked that you cover him, and that you hide not yourself from [the needs of] your own flesh and blood? Then shall your light break forth as the morning, and your healing [your restoration and the power of a new life] shall spring forth speedily.

Are you ready to stop focusing on yourself and your circumstances? *If you forget about yourself, don't worry, God will still remember you!* Your obedience will open the way for Him to work on your behalf and your joy will be greater.

A Root of Bitterness

An attractive woman named Kathie sat across the room from me, gripping the arms of her chair. As she told her story, her mouth was tight, her face drawn. "I was just denied a raise!" she exclaimed. "My supervisor told me that my job performance was poor. I've never been good at anything. Every time I try something new, I hear my mother's voice reminding me how stupid I am. I fail at everything. I'll *never* be successful."

As we continued to talk, it became evident that Kathie's mother had badly abused her. It also became evident that Kathie was making little effort to succeed.

She had a record of poor work attendance, she failed to meet deadlines and she had an uncooperative attitude.

When I challenged Kathie with these facts, she replied, "Well, I know that, but you see if I ever really did become successful, my mother would feel absolved of the guilt for the abuse. She would believe that she hadn't really harmed me after all."

Because Kathie had invested her life into proving that she was a victim of childhood abuse, she was enmeshed in her depression. Her life was not geared toward success. Instead, it was an investment in bitterness, revenge and the desire for satisfaction. As Kathie struggled with the decision to release her bitterness, she cried, "But if I change now I will have wasted thirty years! And my mother will never have to admit that she abused me."

Kathie later developed a physical condition for which she blamed her mother and was not willing to see that she had initiated the condition herself as the outgrowth of her poor mental health.

While Kathie was living her life against her mother, she was also living it against *herself*. If she wanted healing, she would have to give up revenge toward her mother and that was more than she was willing to do. She refused to enter life. She also refused to grow up.

Are you willing to let God show you how decisions about bitterness may be affecting your body? Are you ready to do what is required for healing? If so, you will soon discover that the essential first step is forgiveness.

Forgiveness breaks the bondage of bitterness. I have found that few people know what it means to forgive. Because of our confusion and lack of knowledge, we often retain unnecessary painful connections to other people for years.

When I was in my twenties I was badly hurt by a neighbor. For months I replayed the hurtful scene in my mind, talking about it often with a friend. As I expressed my feelings over and over, my pain became deeper and more invasive. It was slowly becoming part of me.

One day as I was reliving the scene once again, my friend looked me straight in the eye and said, "Do you know that we become like the people we think about the most?" I was startled by her question. It was a wake-up call.

Then God spoke to me from 2 Corinthians 3:18:

> And all of us, as with unveiled face, [because we] continued to behold [in the Word of God] as in a mirror the glory of the Lord, are constantly being transfigured into His very own image in ever increasing splendor and from one degree of glory to another; [for this comes] from the Lord [Who is] the Spirit.

As I read His Word, I realized that I had a choice to make. If I chose to behold Jesus, to focus on Him, I could be transformed into His image. Likewise, if I continued to behold the image of my neighbor, I could be transformed into her image. In fact, that was already happening.

I quickly chose to become like Jesus, but when I realized that my choice involved forgiving my neighbor I became quite resistant. I wanted some satisfaction. I wanted her to admit that she had been unfair and hurtful. I wanted a guarantee that her behavior toward me would change.

Besides, if I forgave her, would she ever realize how hurtful she had been? If I forgave her, would she just assume that I was giving her permission to continue to hurt me? If I forgave her, would I have to include her in special occasions and act as though she was my best friend?

Exactly what does it mean to forgive?

When we forgive someone, it does not mean that those who hurt us will go unpunished. It does, however, mean that God must do the punishing. He wants to choose when, where and how it is done. Romans 12:19 tells us: "Beloved, never avenge yourselves, but leave the way open for [God's] wrath; for it is written, Vengeance is Mine, I will repay (requite), says the Lord."

If we are going to leave the matter in God's hands, we must decide to trust Him. God does not take the hurts of His children lightly. If He says that He will repay, He will repay.

Then if we forgive, do we have to submit ourselves to continual mistreatment? Absolutely not! Living like a victim does not glorify God. He is glorified when we let Him deliver us from harm. Psalm 34:19 says: "Many evils confront the [consistently] righteous; but the Lord delivers him out of them all." If you need deliverance, forgive those who have harmed you and He will deliver you.

When we forgive, we must give up the desire for revenge. Most of us like to talk about getting revenge, but we seldom do anything. If we are not actually going to *do anything,* why not let God do as He pleases? Then we can move on with life. The heavy burden of bitterness will be gone and joy can take its place.

Even if the one who has hurt us never changes, we will not become like him or her. We will be free to become like Jesus, and that is quite a reward for our obedience!

I did decide to forgive my neighbor, as you have probably surmised. God soon provided a time for me to tell her how I felt, and we were able to reach some important agreements that changed our relationship. I did not become transformed into her image, and she did not remain trapped in it, either. We were both free to begin again and we both became more like Jesus.

Are you ready to forgive those who have harmed you? Are you ready to take joy instead of bitterness?

Ignorance and Arrogance

A priest once said to me, "I've been depressed for years. I've asked God over and over to remove this affliction from me and He just doesn't do it." Sensing this man's despair, I asked, "Are you aware that there are many medications available today for depression?"

The priest replied, "Yes, I am. Doctors have tried to get me on those medications for years, but I think that I should be able to conquer this through prayer."

It is my belief that God had already sent the priest an answer: It was in the pharmacy on the corner. However, he let his ignorance and spiritual pride keep him from going to get it.

A friend, Theba, expressed similar thoughts: "After having been tired and apathetic for months, I finally went to see a doctor. I thought that I might be depressed but because my father had experienced depression to the point of suicide attempts, I had been afraid to face the possibility that I might be depressed, too. After my doctor completed his examination, he casually slid in the word *depression*. I heard what he said and my stomach tightened. No! I wasn't going to give in. As we continued to talk I battled with pride and anger. I thought, *Christians don't take anti-depressants. It's a sign of giving up, an indication of little faith.*

"The next morning as I sat at the kitchen table with my roommates, I strained to voice the words that I had run from all my life: 'I'm depressed and I think I need medication.' Just the thought that I might be depressed sent me into a state of fear, and as I waited for their disapproving reaction my accelerated heartbeats braced for the worst. Expecting rejection and shame, I thought, *Would they lose their confidence in my ability to live a Christian life? Would they see me as just some troubled person with whom they will have to bear? How could this happen to me?* I felt like such a failure."

As Theba began taking her medication, she continued to battle with shame and the fear of rejection. However, as weeks passed she began to feel better. She was able to sleep. Her energy level rose and she began to look forward to each new day. Through counseling she was able to address the causes of her depression. She learned to avoid the pitfalls that her father had not recognized. In several months she was able to discontinue the medication and lead a normal life.

"I almost let my fear of depression deprive me of the cure for it!" she exclaimed. "I came so close to repeating the cycle of my father's misery. Now I feel that I have been rescued and given a new start."

When we try to dictate what avenue of healing we will accept, we are likely to trap ourselves in our current conditions, refusing to take help that God has *already* made available.

Are there methods for healing that you have disregarded? Do you need to get more information? Are you knowledgeable enough to make a good decision? Are you willing to try the options that God has already provided for you? If so, get started now.

Toxic Emotions

Luke 6:45 tells us that out of the heart the mouth speaks. Listen to the following statements and see if any of them are familiar to you.

"He makes my blood boil!"

"When I'm around her, I get a knot in my stomach."

"This is a backbreaking job."

"She makes me want to gag!"

"I just can't swallow that."

"He broke my health when he left."

"Just thinking about what happened takes my breath away."

"You scared the life out of me!"

"He's a pain in the neck!"

"I really think this is going to kill me."

"I'll never live through this."

When we make such statements, not only are we expressing the emotions behind them but we are giving our bodies those messages as signals and it responds accordingly.

When you become angry, for instance, what does your body do? Does your pulse race, your face become flushed? Do your muscles tighten? Does your voice become higher, your words coming faster and faster? Do you pace? When you are angry every part of your body comes into action to help you express it; thus, both your mind and body become "angry." In this sense is it possible that your emotions are overloading your body and making it sick?

Years ago when my mother was struggling with depression, she came to stay at our house for a week. The tense atmosphere in our home left me feeling continuously anxious. At midweek I broke out in an itchy rash all over my body. I said to my husband, "I must be allergic to something. What do you think it could be?" He smiled, and said, "Honey, that's an easy answer. You're allergic to your mother." He was right! When my mother left my anxiety level came down and my rash went away on the same day.

Are you willing for God to show you how your emotions may be affecting the health of your body? Are you ready to know what is required for relief? If you are, listen to the words that you speak. Notice how your body cooperates with you to express your emotions. Ask God to show you how to change your emotional responses so that your body may recover. Become willing to change your attitudes.

Complaining and the Importance of Praise

In Jeremiah 15:18 God speaks a strong word to Jeremiah about his attitude. What had gone wrong with this great prophet of God? See if you can recognize an attitude that is common to us all in Jeremiah's words: "Why is my pain perpetual, and my wound incurable, refusing to be healed? Will you indeed be to me as a deceitful brook, like waters that fall and are uncertain?" Do you hear Jeremiah's attitude of self-pity and distrust?

As Jeremiah accuses God of being unfaithful to him, God replies with these words: "If you return [give up this mistaken tone of distrust and despair], then I will give you again a settled place of quiet and safety, and you shall be My minister; and if you separate the precious from the vile [cleansing your own heart from *unworthy suspicions* concerning God's faithfulness], you shall be as My mouthpiece" (verse 19, emphasis added).

God was telling Jeremiah that his complaining attitude was keeping him from receiving the benefits of God's faithfulness. Can you remember times that you have felt exactly like Jeremiah?

When you are suffering, although it may be extremely difficult, it is important to constantly remember the past blessings that God has given you. Look at the words of David: "O my God, my life is cast down upon me [and I find the burden more than I can bear]; therefore will I [earnestly] remember You" (Psalm 42:6).

I believe that it is almost impossible to receive anything from someone we resent. Wasn't God asking Jeremiah to stop complaining and to fix his eyes on His greatness and healing power? Wasn't He showing him the pathway to healing?

If you have been complaining against God, are you ready to stop? If you remember the love God has poured out on you, along with His gracious mercy to you in the past, will you begin to praise Him again? If you are ready, begin now. Open yourself to receive from Him.

Confusion About the Will of God

Robin, a young woman suffering from depression, told me this about her experience of growing up: "My mother and my grandmother were depressed. They constantly bemoaned their emotional condition, telling me, 'You'll be depressed someday, too, just wait and see. Your time will come, but remember: God never gives you more than you can bear. There's a purpose in it. You'll just have to endure it, but trials make us stronger.'"

Robin's mother, as well as her grandmother, taught her that their depression was from God created to produce character. Because of her false belief, Robin had done what they had instructed her to do: She had simply borne it believing that depression was God's will. Because of the emotional pain and fatigue that depression brings, Robin had missed much out of life. Her prolonged anger over her losses had simply put the last nail in her emotional coffin, perpetuating the depression.

Many of us believe as Robin did that God puts mental or physical sickness upon us for our good. It is true, as we have seen, that illness may come as the result of sin. But it is also true that as we turn from sin it is God's pleasure to restore us. Psalm 119:67 tells us: "Before I was afflicted I went astray, but now Your Word do I keep [hearing, receiving, loving and obeying it]." So if you have sinned and have been forgiven, what good effect can sickness have? Robin's depression was not a blessing from God. Through the error she had inherited from her mother and grandmother, Robin had denied herself healing.

As she began to recover, Robin still had some confusion. "In some ways," she said, "I have become stronger during this depression. Will I continue to grow if I get well? I want to be close to God."

While it is true that growth comes during our difficulties, we should not voluntarily maintain an illness in order to try to grow in Christ. If the growth that God had in mind for you has been accomplished, what further good can the sickness do? And when should we be the judges of that? God has many creative ways to motivate us to grow and it is not up to us to design or prolong them.

Will you ask God to teach you how to discern His will? Are you ready to look at opinions or false beliefs that others may have passed on to you and exchange them for the truth?

It is amazing to me how we attribute motives and actions to God that we also attribute to criminals. Once I asked an incest survivor named Anna if she believed that it had been God's will for her to be molested. She immediately replied, "Yes, I do. I believe He let it happen so that I would know how to help other incest survivors when I grew up." I then asked her if she loved or trusted God, and she replied, "No, I don't. Who could love or trust a God like that?" And she had an excellent point. In her mind, there was no difference between the character and actions of God and those of a perpetrator of sexual abuse. No wonder she could not love or trust Him.

As we continued our conversation, Anna came to understand that God had not willed her abuse: the perpetrator had. Because God condemns incest in His Word, she was able to see that God had not willed for her to be molested. God's will for her had been safety.

Anna had misunderstood a critical piece of information. Because God gave us all free will, we can choose to live in ways that harm ourselves and others. *Since God has all power, we make the mistake of believing that He uses it to control us and the world we live in.* The truth is that we live in a fallen environment, as well as among fallen people, and *by our own choices* we harm the earth and one another.

Some of these choices are accidents, mistakes, deliberate mistreatment, carelessness, greed and immorality. We need to be careful that, when we attempt to find meaning in our suffering, we do not give God credit for the evil in our lives. *He is our Deliverer from evil, not the perpetrator of it and its consequences.*

Are you ready to ask God to speak truth to you about your condition? To ask Him to reveal His will for you? If you are, be ready to give up false beliefs and begin a new walk with Him.

The Big Question

As you undertake the challenge of removing blocks to healing you may be asking yourself, "What if I address my blocks to healing and I am still not healed?" Let me ask you another question. How many people do you know who have peace of mind? Would you like to be one of them? Wherever you may be in your journey toward healing, addressing these blocks will bring you closer to God and you will become a person of peace and truth. You will be stronger in spirit and you will not be defeated in life. Whether you are sick or well, God can empower you: A person of peace and truth cannot be stopped.

As you remove the blocks that could cause you to stumble, you will see that nothing can stand in the way of the Healer and His will for you.

Suggested Prayer

Father, please help me. Show me if there are any blocks to my healing. Please release me from guilt and shame. I am willing to do whatever You ask of me, no matter how difficult it may be. Enable me to trust You. I completely humble myself before You and surrender myself into Your care.

Please reveal truth about my relationships. Enable me to forgive those who have harmed me, and give me the courage to seek forgiveness of those whom I have harmed. Teach me to forgive myself. Fill my heart with love for You, myself and others. Let Your perfect love cast out all of my fears.

As I read Your Word, listen for Your Voice and walk each day with You, please pour Your healing power into my mind, body and spirit. I want to receive from You, Lord, and I want to give You glory for all that You do in me. Amen.

2

SEARCHING
FOR THE WILL OF GOD

In 1991, after having been healthy most of my life, I became sick with a condition that was not diagnosed correctly for almost two years. When the pain first began I simply expected to go to a doctor, be diagnosed, take medicine and get well.

After the pain continued for several months, I saw clearly that I had been naive concerning the process of my recovery. I was forced to enter the complicated maze of today's medical profession. Weeks turned into months and my pain intensified. I felt as if I had entered another world, one of suffering, confusion and uncertainty. As I waited in doctors' offices, I would look around at others whose bodies were bent with pain. *What am I doing here?* I would pray silently. *Lord, please heal me.*

My pleasantly passing days as Recovery Director of a shelter for battered or homeless women and children gradually gave way to endless hours of waiting between medical tests and procedures. I experienced no relief from suffering. My condition became a mystery illness signified by intense abdominal pain.

My mild-mannered husband felt helpless to relieve my suffering. One day when he became especially distressed by my pain, he said, "Honestly, it makes me angry to see you working so hard to help others when God isn't doing anything to help you!" Pain is exhausting. Both he and I were tired, confused and feeling angry because there had been no relief. It seemed as if there would be no end to our misery.

At the end of the first year, increasing pain forced me to resign from my job. I began to experience the emotions that come with prolonged illness: discouragement, confusion, frustration, lack of control and false guilt. I felt overwhelmed because I could not keep up at work. When I came home, I felt guilty because I could not keep up my responsibilities there either. Because of the pain I could not even pick up my grandchild. Life was closing in.

As I watched the energetic, busy lives of my friends and associates I was envious. I began to get a glimpse of the serious effects an illness could have on every area of my life—not only physical but also emotional, financial and social. And still I had no answers.

Life felt uncertain. I remember saying, "I feel as though my entire life is tentative." I found myself unable to commit to anything, saying, "I will if I can when the time comes." If you have experienced this uncertainty, you know what chaos it can create. You know that we truly learn to live only one day or moment at a time. I learned to pray, "Jesus, just show me the next step."

I also learned that the greatest need for those who are sick is not for sympathy or pat answers. Compassion and understanding are helpful, but the greatest need is for relief of pain, emotional or physical, and to believe that it is God's will for us to recover and be restored to health. I needed hope. If you or someone you love is suffering, you need hope as well.

What Is God's Will in This?

One day a friend asked me, "Do you believe that it is God's will for you to get well?" Although I had studied healing in the Scriptures for years I had to confess to my friend that I had grown uncertain. On the one hand, if I did not believe that it was God's will for me to recover, why was I going to so many doctors? If healing was not God's will, was I not just involving some well-meaning physicians in defying Him? And yet, on the other hand, nothing was helping. I had no relief, no assurance that He wanted me to get well.

Then I read James 1:6–8, a familiar passage, which says,

> It must be in faith that he asks, with no wavering—no hesitating, no doubting. For the one who wavers (hesitates, doubts) is like the billowing surge out at sea, that is blown hither and thither and tossed by the wind. For truly, let not such a person imagine that he will receive anything [he asks for] from the Lord, [for being as he is] a man of two minds—hesitating, dubious, irresolute—[he is] unstable and unreliable and uncertain about everything (he thinks, feels, decides).

As I read those words I knew that I definitely needed spiritual clarity! I came to realize that my ambivalence was a constant drain. I knew that I would not have the stamina to continue any kind of search if I had a divided mind. Remembering some of the words from Psalm 25, I prayed, "Teach me Your ways, show me Your path and give me an undivided heart."

By that time the doctors were giving up the search for a cure. "We think you are just going to have to find a way to live with this pain," they said. I had been to more than a dozen specialists. I desperately needed to know if God really wanted me to get well or not.

Asking the Holy Spirit to be my Guide, I began again to search the Scriptures, proving once again that faith takes root when we seek guidance from God's Word. After all, is it not what He says to us that makes the biggest difference? I began to get quiet and hear Him. It did not take long for Him to reach my heart.

Jehovah Rapha, Our Doctor

I began my search in the Old Testament where God first introduced Himself as our Healer. Speaking to Moses and the Israelites, He said,

> If you will diligently hearken to the voice of the Lord your God, and will do what is right in His sight, and will listen to and obey His commandments and keep all His statutes, I will put none of the diseases upon you which I brought upon the Egyptians; *for I am the Lord Who heals you.*
>
> EXODUS 15:26 (EMPHASIS ADDED)

The word used for *Lord* in this verse is *rapha,* the Hebrew word for "doctor." That settled it for me. I decided that our Father wants healing for us. Why would He present Himself to us as our Doctor if He did not want to heal us?

I began to pray to my Doctor, asking Him for my healing. I realized that His promise was conditional upon my obedience to His ways. I asked the Holy Spirit to help me make an inventory of my life. I wanted nothing left standing between my Doctor and me that could hinder His readiness to heal me. In fact, I followed the Twelve-Step program of Alcoholics Anonymous. I asked God to reveal any unconfessed sin or areas in which I had neglected to make restitution for wrongs done. I made a list of people to contact and I called each of them. I wanted to be free of any guilt, anger, worry, fear or shame that might sap the energy that my body could use toward healing.

The Scripture that had the greatest impact on me at this time was Isaiah 53:4–5:

> Surely He has borne our griefs—sickness, weakness and distress—and carried our sorrows and pains [of punishment]. . . . But He was wounded for our transgressions, He was bruised for our guilt and iniquities; the chastisement needful to obtain peace and well-being for us was upon Him, and *with the stripes that wounded Him we are healed and made whole.*
>
> (EMPHASIS ADDED)

I prayed over that passage of Scripture, asking God to teach me about His healing power and His will for healing. I asked Him to give me faith to endure. I asked Him to reveal Himself to me as Jehovah Rapha.

As I began to know my God as my Healer, my desire to draw closer to Him increased. I wanted not only to receive my healing but also to receive His compassion and Presence. I began daily to proclaim Psalm 103:1, 3 which says: "Bless—affectionately, gratefully praise—the Lord, O my soul, and all that is [deepest] within me, bless His holy name! . . . Who forgives [every one of] all your iniquities, Who heals [each of] all your diseases."

After many days of study in the Old Testament, I turned to the book of Matthew. In chapter eight I found that Jesus healed a leper, the paralyzed servant of the centurion, Peter's mother-in-law and people who were bound by demonic spirits. Amid the accounts of those healings were these words: "And thus He fulfilled what was spoken by the prophet Isaiah, He Himself took (in order to carry away) our weaknesses and infirmities and bore away our diseases" (Matthew 8:17).

When He walked on earth Jesus Himself said, "I have come down from heaven, not to do My own will and purpose; but to do the will and purpose of Him Who sent me" (John 6:38). It was obvious that Jesus was doing His Father's will as He healed people.

What About Paul's Thorn?

I continued to study, pray and wait for healing, growing more confident in Jesus' desire to continue healing today. Each day I would ground myself in faith by writing out Scriptures, building faith to receive from Him. Romans 10:17 tells us that faith comes by hearing the Word of God.

It was a positive and hopeful time, yet a thought nagged at me. What about Paul's "thorn in the flesh"? I wondered often about his ongoing affliction. I had never really cared to study 2 Corinthians 12:7–9 where God told Paul that He will not heal him. In fact, I avoided that particular passage for almost two years!

But I could ignore it no longer. It was beginning to appear as though I was being medically condemned as beyond healing. The last specialist said, "Lynda, you are simply going to have to learn to live with this. There are no more tests to be run, no more medications to try . . . and no one knows what is wrong with you." I was at a crossroads; it appeared that there was nothing more anyone could do. I was drawn to the "dreaded passage."

As I began to read, however, I realized two things that I had never thought about before. First, it was clear that although God denied healing to Paul, He fully supplied all of his needs. He said, "My grace—My favor and loving kindness and mercy are enough for you . . . for My strength and power are made perfect—fulfilled and completed and show themselves most effective in [your] weakness."

Thus, as I studied Paul's life further, I found that in spite of his affliction he was able to travel, to preach, to do miracles and to perform signs and wonders. He was also able to endure prison and to write a great portion of the New Testament. In fact, Paul said that "when I am weak (in human strength), then am I [truly] strong—able, powerful in divine strength" (2 Corinthians 12:10), and "I have *not fallen short one bit* or *proved myself at all inferior*" (2 Corinthians 12:11, emphasis added). Paul rejoiced when he saw the way that God's power could compensate for his personal loss of abilities.

Second, and even more encouraging for me, was the fact that even though God told Paul that He would not heal him, He gave him a direct answer. He did not keep Paul in suspense about his condition. At that point in my life, considering my condition and the prognosis of my doctor, I needed a direct answer desperately. I was at the end of my emotional road. I had to have a word from Him concerning my condition. So I prayed, "Father, even if You are not going to heal me, I need an answer. Just tell me the truth. If You want me to have this pain the rest of my life, please tell me so that I can stop searching for healing and begin to adjust to a different way of living. I need for You to give me a blessing of assurance as you gave Paul. I need to know that I will be able to fulfill the purposes of my life. I promise to serve You, whether I am sick or well."

After my prayer, there was a difference. Throughout my search I had experienced great anxiety. Now I felt a perfect peace. I knew that, even if my pain never ceased, I would be able to bear it and accomplish the purposes God had for me.

Do you have that kind of peace? Are you still anxious as I was? If you are, remember that peace always follows total surrender.

A Breakthrough

About two weeks after my prayer a friend told me about a 69-year-old neurosurgeon who might be able to help me. Because of his age and experience, I thought that this doctor might have seen cases like mine. When I told my husband that I wanted to see another doctor, he asked me if I was sure that I could go through the process all over again, having faced so many disappointments. I understood his feelings, but the peace I was experiencing seemed to bring a new level of faith. I decided to make one last appointment.

As I drove to the doctor's office, I felt a surge of anticipation and excitement. I experienced an unusual level of confidence as I walked into the waiting room. The doctor listened carefully to my description of symptoms and studied my MRI reports. Then he told me that he had seen only a few cases like mine in more than forty years of practice. He informed me that he did not believe that my pain came from a diseased organ but from a neurological problem caused by a congenital defect in my spine. After a few procedures to confirm his diagnosis, he scheduled surgery for me as soon as possible. The day of my deliverance from pain came the day before Thanksgiving. How appropriate!

As the nurses prepared me for surgery, one expressed regret that I would have to be in the hospital for Thanksgiving. I told her, "There is nothing to be sorry about. This is truly Thanksgiving for me." I wanted to be nowhere else except in the surgery room. I felt absolutely convinced that the cause of my pain had been found, and that surgery would bring my healing. I had no fear and my anticipation of complete healing was at an all-time high.

The surgery was successful. The doctor found a broken disk that had compressed nerves leading to internal organs, creating nerve pain and internal spasms. The ragged edge of the disk had almost completely severed a tendon across my lower back. The doctor removed the disk, the tendon healed and within two months, I was pain-free at last. How I praised God for the release!

Now, every day is a new start, as I continually give thanks to Him for giving me my freedom.

Evidence of Jesus' Desire to Heal

Are you aware that Jesus spent approximately one-third of His ministry healing people? Matthew 9:35–36, one of the many passages that gave me hope, tells us that Jesus was moved by pity and sympathy for the sick because He saw that they were helpless—like sheep without a shepherd. Jesus never turned anyone away because his disease was too serious (leprosy) or because he had been sick for too long (the man at the pool) or because of the sick person's sins (the crippled man). Jesus healed men, women, old people, young people and children of various afflictions. It appears that when sick people came to Jesus, they were granted healing just as sinners were who sought salvation, if they obeyed His commands. In fact, are you aware that the word *salvation* according to *Strong's Concordance* means "to deliver, protect, preserve, to heal and make whole"?

The significance of Jesus' willingness to heal any disease was emphasized to me by a friend named Bill who had suffered with prostate cancer for four years. Bill's original diagnosis was "late stage, aggressive and inoperable." The statistics gave only a thirty percent chance of his living more than five years.

At age 54, with a wonderful wife and seven-year-old daughter, a thriving business, and a robust social and spiritual life, Bill told me he felt as though everything in his life that had finally fallen into place was now being blown apart. While dealing with the devastation, he began a four-point program of wellness, including conventional medical treatment, a support group, alternative approaches to healing cancer and a heavy intake of God's Word. Bill began searching through the Bible diligently, looking for God's "heart" toward us concerning health and well-being.

While it went well for most of those four years, his oncologist finally told Bill that the drugs that had been successful thus far had lost their effect. There were few options left short of chemotherapy. "I feared the phase of this terrible disease that would lead to the decision regarding chemo," said Bill, "which is not very effective on prostate cancer." Suffering and death seemed inevitable.

Bill again descended into the depths of despair and doubt, wondering what God could be up to, how He could be so distant in such a present need. He restudied the hundreds of verses he had marked with *c* for "cancer battle" in his Bible. Bill said that he gained some victory over doubt and anxiety, but the core level of fear persisted.

"Finally, in desperation," he said, "I put all other interests aside and began a search to know, to really know Jesus as Healer. To do this, I began in Matthew, noting how Jesus Christ reacted to diseased people as He moved among them. I also began reading through Luke, reasoning that this doctor would have some enlightening words on Jesus as Healer."

Bill said that a major turning point came for him when he reread Matthew 8–9, for here Jesus is revealed as the Healer as He is nowhere else. Bill underlined the following sentences in his Bible (from the New International Version):

- "Lord, if you are willing, you can make me clean." Jesus reached out his hand and touched the man. "I am willing," he said. "Be clean!" Immediately he was cured.
- Jesus said to him, "I will go and heal him."
- Then Jesus said to the centurion, "Go! It will be done just as you believed it would." And his servant was healed at that very hour.

- When evening came, many who were demon-possessed were brought to him and he drove out the spirits with a word and healed all the sick. This was to fulfill what was spoken through the prophet Isaiah: "He took up our infirmities and carried our diseases."
- Jesus turned and saw her. "Take heart, daughter," he said, "your faith has healed you."
- Jesus went through all of the towns and villages, teaching in their synagogues, preaching the good news of the kingdom and healing every disease and sickness.

Bill said, "As I continued my study, I found that an unmistakable portrait of our Lord had been painted in clear sight on the pages of Scripture! Before this I had always pictured Him as reluctant to heal, as having to be convinced." Bill wrote these conclusions in the margin of his Bible:

- Jesus is not reluctant to heal when faith is exercised in Him as Healer.
- Healing was tied to the faith of the seeking person or of those seeking healing on someone else's behalf. Faith was a necessity, not an option.
- There is no instance of Jesus refusing to heal on either theological grounds or the fear of too much faith being placed in Him. The Scriptures clearly record His willingness and readiness to heal.
- Everything in Matthew 8–9 encourages faith in Jesus as Healer. There is no discouragement or warning that He will not or does not heal.

As Bill and I concluded our conversation, he said, "Healing is about Him, His Person, His power and His presence. Healing is in Him, and it is in knowing Him that we are healed. He is life and power over evil and death. He hates sickness and takes every opportunity to do away with it. In fact, our prayer should be, 'Lord, I surrender totally.' That is when life and healing really come."

When I asked Bill about his current physical condition, he replied that tests show his PSA reading, an indication of the severity of the cancer, to have dropped to a normal range, much to the astonishment of his doctor.

"Does this mean my battle is completely over? I don't know; it may be and it may not be," he said. "But one thing is certain: Jesus Christ the Healer lives and will be present to respond to faith and dependence on Him, regardless of any reading. He shall forever remain my Hope and my Healer."

Would you like to be one who believes, too? Will you do as Bill did and enmesh yourself in His Word and ask that Jesus be revealed as your Healer? Will you believe Him, knowing that He is Your Hope? If you will, begin now.

The Healing Gift of the Holy Spirit

It seems surprising, but many believers still ask, "Who is the Holy Spirit?" The Holy Spirit, the third Person of the Trinity, is God on the earth with us today, the One who lives within us and works God's purposes in our lives. God the Father is in heaven (see Matthew 6:9); Jesus sits at His right hand (see Hebrews 10:12); and the Holy Spirit is the One Jesus sent to be with us (see John 16:7–8; Acts 1:5).

On occasion I will hear someone say, "If only we had lived in Jesus' day, we could have seen Him face-to-face and watched the miracles. Then it would be easy to believe for healing." If you feel that way, too, imagine how you would respond if Jesus suddenly appeared in the flesh while you were working or reading or resting today. Wouldn't you be awestruck? Wouldn't you bow down in worship and gratitude? Wouldn't you humbly make your request for healing? Do you realize that you can do that now? If you are a believer, Jesus lives in you by the power of the Holy Spirit. And the Spirit is as fully God as Jesus. His power is by no means diminished because you cannot see or touch Him. The Holy Spirit *is* God and He is there with you. He is the One who does the work of healing in your body.

If someone has a miracle healing, for instance, beyond medical capabilities or the normal restorative nature of the body—itself a wonderful gift from our heavenly Father!—that is the work of the Holy Spirit. And whereas Jesus could be only at one place at a time, healing one person at a time, God through the Holy Spirit is available to tend to the needs of all who call on Him . . . *all at the same time.*

One day after waiting for several hours in a doctor's office, I said quietly, "Thank you, Holy Spirit, that I do not have to make an appointment with You! I don't have to be put on Your patient list, and I don't have to wait in line to see You. I can always be top priority with You." I realized that no one else's case could take precedence over mine with the Holy Spirit, because He is capable of helping everyone who is sick all at once. No appointments necessary! *Even though He is invisible, He is always available.*

First Corinthians 12 tells us that when the Holy Spirit was poured out, God made special gifts available to His people. One of these was the gift of healing, that those who receive it might be particularly anointed to help those who are suffering. James 5:13–16 advises us to call for elders of the church to lay hands on the sick. He assures us that prayer is dynamic in its working, and the sick may be healed and restored.

A good friend of mine, Carolyn, related the way a healing gift was poured out on her. She said, "For many years I lived in secret despair, an alcoholic housewife. In my heart I cried out to God, for I never doubted that He existed. I had not experienced His power because I had insisted on demanding answers for *my* life in *my* way."

Carolyn explained that she began to drink in college. After a drink or two she was able to become the person she longed to be—warm, friendly, popular. Soon she lost control over her drinking and it controlled her. By the time she admitted to herself that she was an alcoholic, she had married, had a child, divorced and remarried.

"We moved to a new town and suddenly I was thrown with people who lived happy, satisfied lives without alcohol," she said. "This was staggering to me, and for the first time I began to face the fact that I really might have a drinking problem. I sought the help of a psychiatrist and I joined AA. I was still not able to stop drinking. I had also become a chain smoker.

"Many wonderful Christians prayed for me when I joined a church, seeking help there. I condemned myself daily, asking how I could consider myself a Christian when I couldn't stay sober even one day. I was in that desperate condition for two years, and I loathed myself."

At one point, through sheer determination, Carolyn went three months without a cigarette or alcohol. The need for a drink was growing, however. She knew she would fall again. It was just a matter of time.

"One night at church," Carolyn said, "a woman approached me after the service was over asking if I needed prayer. I sensed somehow that her offer was sent to me from God. We moved into a small adjoining room and she laid hands on me, praying that I would be delivered from the bondage of alcohol. Although I experienced no intense emotion or physical sensations, I left the church in perfect peace, believing for the first time that I would be set free. That night, as I prepared for bed, I pulled my blouse over my head and a strong smell of alcohol and tobacco reeked from it. Since it had been three months since I had indulged in either, I concluded that this was just another work of God, cleansing my body as He had cleansed my soul.

"This happened to me more than thirty years ago, and my life has been totally transformed. The desire to drink has never returned. All of the energy I had been using to suppress my unholy, addictive desires is now used in a positive direction. How I thank God for setting me free!"

It is obvious that the Holy Spirit made a divine appointment with Carolyn, touching her through someone with a special gift, releasing His dynamic power, breaking the bondage over her life.

Are you aware of the healing gift of the Holy Spirit? Would you like to pray to receive this gift? Do you need someone who has this gift of healing to pray with you? Remember that the Holy Spirit is available to you at any time. Ask God to help you through the work and ministry of the Holy Spirit.

The Healing Power in the Blood of Christ

One of my favorite movies is the classic *Ben Hur*. Do you remember one of the last scenes in the movie when three women sought shelter from the storm after the crucifixion? Two of the women had come too late to receive the healing from Jesus they sought. Disappointed, they ran into a cave when the thunder and lightning began. Do you remember seeing the blood of Jesus pouring down from His body as He hung on the cross? Do you recall the astonishment of the two leprous women when they saw that they were healed as the blood began to flow? Do you remember their wonder and joy? As they rejoiced, the flow of the blood increased and mingled with the rain pouring down on the earth. This scene presents a graphic picture of the spiritual reality that we can experience today if we understand the entire purpose of the cross: Jesus' death not only secured our salvation but our healing.

A woman named Sandra who was recovering from a heart condition told me, "I knew that when Jesus saved me He gave me eternal life, but I didn't realize He offered me healing, too. Now I see that He doesn't want me to remain sick any more than He wanted me to remain lost! Since I have understood the entire truth about my salvation, I am gaining the same confidence about getting well that I have about going to heaven. I am much more motivated now to follow through on my treatment, exercising and watching my diet. I truly believe that I will receive complete healing."

The Meaning of the Cross

Someone once said to me, "I have thought about people who suffer or die for others, such as those who give their lives in wars. Of course, I've always appreciated what Jesus did on the cross, but I've also wondered if He really suffered any more than other heroes did." The answer to that is yes, He did. The difference between the suffering of war heroes and Jesus is that war heroes suffered their own pain and death. Not only did Jesus suffer His own physical pain, but He bore the sin of everyone who has ever lived or ever will live, as well as the effects of those sins—separation from God.

Hebrews 9:12 says: "He went once for all into the [Holy of] Holies [of heaven], not by virtue of the blood of goats and calves . . . but His own blood, having found and secured a complete redemption—an everlasting release [for us]."

No other human could—or *would*—do that for us. The "exchanges" of the cross make true release possible for us. We can exchange sickness for health, weakness for His strength, our distresses for peace, our sorrows for joy, and our guilt for cleansing and forgiveness.

During my illness I had to face my anger toward God for allowing my pain to continue for so long. I knew that I needed the blood of Jesus to cleanse my heart. Only the perfect sacrifice could release me from the bitterness that I felt.

First Peter 1:19 refers to the blood of Jesus as "the precious blood . . . like that of a [sacrificial] lamb without blemish or spot." As I came to understand the extent of Jesus' provision for us, I loved Him more than ever. How could we not love Someone who cared enough to identify with us and meet every need that we would ever have?

Have you ever thought about the fact that the blood of Jesus flowed through the body of someone who never had an evil thought? The effects of toxic emotions, such as prolonged anger or bitterness or guilt and shame, never contaminated His body. His mind and body were surrendered to the Father and He did not experience guilt or regret. He knew total peace. His entire being was free from sin and its effects. Never was any sacrifice perfect enough to atone for my sin until His blood was shed for me!

If you could look into the past and see all of the animals that were ever sacrificed for sin and its effects, you would see an endless slaughter. If their blood were placed in containers, you would never see the end of them. Hebrews 10:10 tells us that, since the blood of Christ was the perfect sacrifice, we were forgiven once and for all. We were granted the opportunity for restoration and wholeness.

What If . . .

Imagine my telling you that archaeologists had just discovered a container holding precious drops of Jesus' blood from the crucifixion. What if I told you it had been so carefully preserved that it was just as pure now as it was then? Would you want to have the blood sprinkled on you? I certainly would! I would want to receive all of its healing effects. Do you realize that we can, even though the actual blood is no longer visible to us? The power of the blood of Jesus has never ceased, and the benefits are delivered to us daily by the power of the Holy Spirit. It is still being poured out and we receive its effects by faith (see 1 John 1:7). *Like the Holy Spirit, the power of the blood is in no way diminished just because we cannot see it. It will never lose its power, and it is always available for those who ask in faith.*

Would you like to receive all of the healing effects of the blood of Christ today? It is the perfect sacrifice. It has been poured out for you and me.

How Did My Illness Work for Good?

James 1:2–4 says this:

> Consider it wholly joyful, my brethren, whenever you are enveloped in or encounter trials of any sort, or fall into various temptations. Be assured and understand that the trial and proving of your faith bring out endurance and steadfastness and patience. But let endurance and steadfastness and patience have full play and do a thorough work, so that you may be [people] perfectly and fully developed (with no defects), lacking in nothing.

A wise pastor once said to me, "If you go through a trial, be sure that you come out of it with something. Let God change you. Gain wisdom. Learn to wait, but come out of it with something good." His words came back to me many times during my two years of trial. It was encouraging to me to know that there was such potential for growth during the difficult times. I felt as if the ground of my soul was being plowed. It was very unpleasant, and there were days I thought I would not be alive by the time the plow reached the end of my row.

A friend recently asked me, "How did those two years of pain change you?" Because I had been careful to search for the treasures of growth within myself, I could give her a ready answer. "One big change is evident," I said. "Before the trial began, I loved being with people more than I loved being alone with God. When I was confined,

I had no other choice but to spend the time alone with God. I learned that there is no better company. Isn't it pathetic that it took something like an illness to discipline me and teach me how wonderful He is?"

I told her that if the president of our country called and invited me to the White House, I would recognize immediately what a special invitation that was. I would begin preparing for my trip. I would not miss that visit for the world. How small such an opportunity is compared to the invitation from Jesus Christ to spend time with Him! Now, I *prefer* my times alone with Him. He is first choice.

I continued. "And another thing. I have always been an extremely enthusiastic person. Waiting for God's direction was difficult for me. In fact, I did *not* always wait and more than once found myself paying the price for my impulsive actions. That changed, as did the area of overworking. I used to put my whole heart into whatever task I faced. I wasn't always willing to discipline myself to keep life in a healthy balance. I believe that all of these traits, along with the congenital birth defect in my spine, may have directly precipitated the trial of my illness. But whether they did or not, I have changed my ways. I no longer enjoy being on overload, driven by the adrenaline of a fast-forwarded life, and I have seen that seeking God's direction saves a lot of heartache."

My friend smiled and I realized in a flash that my former traits had been obvious to those who were close to me all the time!

These are just some of the good things that came out of those two years. Psalm 119:67 says: "Before I was afflicted I went astray, but now Your word do I keep [hearing, receiving, loving and obeying it]." I have come to see that there are some things you cannot make up your mind to change; the change has to be performed within you by the Holy Spirit. The pressure we face in trials is a great catalyst for change, as well as the perfect avenue to humility.

Are there changes God has spoken to you about for a long time? Perhaps you will slow down and listen more than I did and will be able to avoid a time of trial. If, however, you find that the pressures of a trial are upon you, submit yourself to God, listen carefully, and as the pastor told me, "Be sure that you come out of it with some good things."

The most important thing I learned through my healing experience is that our God can truly be trusted. I faced so many helpless moments and circumstances I would never have dreamed that I could endure and keep a sound mind. Maybe we only come to know the power of God as we experience it personally. Would I want to go through another time like this one? No, I would not. Do I value my experience? Yes, I value it enormously, because my faith has been increased and deepened. Most of all, I became more closely acquainted with Jehovah Rapha, with Jesus our Healer and with the Holy Spirit and His gifts. I experienced inside my own mind and body the blessings that were given to me through the cross of Jesus Christ. My suffering seems small now compared to the enormity of the blessings I have received.

A New Responsibility—Always Remember

I want to share one more story with you, one told me by a neonatal specialist here in Little Rock named Dr. Terry Zuerlein. It is the story of how he became acquainted with God as Jehovah Rapha. His eyes sparkled with excitement as he told me about Meredith, a 35-year-old woman at high-risk because of bleeding during her pregnancy. It was standard obstetrical procedure to keep her in bed until her baby was delivered in order to minimize the risk of more severe bleeding.

One Friday morning while making the rounds with his patients, Dr. Zuerlein was summoned quickly to the operating room. Meredith's placenta had separated from the uterus and she was bleeding profusely. As Meredith was prepped for surgery, he stood nearby, waiting to resuscitate the newborn infant. "I considered the fragility of life," he told me, "as I remembered Meredith sitting happily in her bed a few hours earlier."

He continued: "The first part of the cesarean section went as usual, but the bleeding became faster than the suction could clear the surgical field. I could see the gravity of concern in the surgeon's eyes as he pulled out a limp, pale little girl and handed her to me. I took her to the infant warmer and began the resuscitation, spending the next few hours fighting for the life of this three-pound-ten-ounce little girl. When she finally began to stabilize, I went to inquire about the mother. I found that her life was in even greater jeopardy than before."

Meredith had received more than thirty units of blood, and even a hysterectomy had not stopped the bleeding. During the next few hours, sixty more units of blood were transfused into her body. Several surgeons worked on her at once, and one even squeezed her aorta with his gloved hand in an attempt to control the hemorrhaging. Her condition deteriorated quickly as her body's systems broke down. Meredith's husband was told that she probably would not make it as no one could survive such bodily trauma.

"At the same moment that I was wondering how such a tragedy could occur," said Dr. Zuerlein, "I remembered having received a bookmark from a friend who had just traveled to the Holy Land the week before. On the bookmark were the words, *Jehovah Rapha the God Who Heals*. I moved to a quiet place and began to call out to Jehovah Rapha on behalf of Meredith. As I sensed His presence, I asked Him to heal Meredith and allow her to recover.

"Approximately twenty minutes later, Meredith's husband found me and told me that Meredith's bleeding had stopped just moments earlier! The attending doctors were astonished at the sudden change in her condition.

Now they were saying that she just might survive after all. A buzz shot up my spine as I witnessed one of the most dramatic healings by God that I had ever imagined possible."

Have you met Jehovah Rapha?

Think about this. Have you ever wondered how many people are healed on the earth every day? How many do you know who have recovered from some physical or emotional illness during the last year? Could you even remember all of them? Even with computers we could never count all of the people in the world each day who leave hospitals and recover. We could never record the number of people who leave the office of a physician, get medications and get well. We will never know how many are healed directly by God's touch as they kneel down and seek Him. Healing is like rain pouring out on thirsty ground. We receive healing over and over. If we will simply take notice, we will see Him confirming His Word at every turn.

Because I earnestly desire to hold onto every ounce of blessing and wisdom I was given during the time of my healing, I refer often to Galatians 5:1, which says: "In [this] freedom Christ has made us free—completely liberated us; stand fast then, and do not be hampered and held ensnared and submit again to a yoke of slavery—which you have once put off."

Many of our spiritual blessings are the prizes of battle. Through our experiences we have learned how to walk a different path than we walked before. It is our responsibility to remember and to live in the light that God has given us. Then we can offer ourselves as well on behalf of others who need Him and need to know His will for healing.

Suggested Prayer

Dear Father, thank You for revealing Yourself as Jehovah Rapha, my Healer. Thank You, Jesus, for

Your sacrifice on the cross. Thank You for the blessings that were poured out to me through Your blood. Help me to understand and receive the healing that You have given me. Holy Spirit, thank You for the many gifts You bring to me every day.

Father, please draw me into Your Word and enable me to see Your truth. Order my thoughts and cause me to choose Your ways. Let me perceive Your will for my life. Spirit of truth, reveal any deceptions that have taken root in my mind. Cause me to see You at work around me. Let truth reign in me. Amen.

3

THE POWER TO ENDURE

Have you ever received bad news and found yourself unwilling or unable to believe it? Did you pretend that the information was not true? When we attempt to buffer ourselves from something we do not want to face, we go into a process called *denial*. Rather than deny the situation, however, it is in these times of severe emotional or physical pain that we must begin to face the truth quickly so that we can prepare ourselves to fight discouragement.

If resolution to your need does not come immediately, you might find yourself facing the anguish of days and nights that seem as if they will never end. There is knowledge, however, that will help you remain strong until your answer comes. During the wait, you will be able to maintain an attitude of faith and gain emotional stability.

Carolyn Anne, having received a distressful call from her doctor following a mammogram, found herself in

71

just such a situation. She told me her story: "Finding a malignancy had been a remote possibility in my mind, but it was definitely not the reality I expected to face. I was stunned. As my mental barriers receded in the face of truth, the diagnosis plunged me into my own Gethsemane.

"I have always been the type who likes life to be smooth and orderly. This illness was a dramatic interruption, making a disarray of my well-scheduled life, ushering in a period of great sorrow, loss and loneliness. I could hardly believe what was happening, but I had to face reality because many decisions needed to be made regarding treatment. The type of cancer that I had was aggressive and fast-growing. Because the cancer was already involving lymph nodes, my physician recommended a complete mastectomy.

"At that point, I felt as if I was trying to swim through a deep emotional ocean, struggling against the tide, fighting frequent undertow. This mental image of my distress continued to plague me until I began to imagine a lighthouse far in the distance. I assured myself that I would eventually arrive at that lighthouse if I just kept swimming. Of course, the lighthouse represented Jesus, safety and health.

"As my treatment was chosen, I began to experience a different level of distress. Because I had always been very health-conscious, it was difficult for me to allow various chemicals to invade my body. I knew that they would bring me healing, but I was also afraid of them. I experienced emotional conflict on every level of my being. My hair began to fall out, and as I looked at my hair lying on the shower floor I offered this entire experience to God for His glory.

"My husband, knowing that I was a very private person, asked me if I would rather not see friends during that time. I decided that I would not isolate myself from the encouragement of friends, although I felt that I looked terrible. The cancer threatened my sense of personal privacy and dignity, but I decided not to hide myself away.

"Early in my treatment, my husband planned a special vacation we would take at the end of my treatment. Having something specific to look forward to helped me remember that life could be normal again, even fun. I constantly looked forward to that time, but I knew we had a long journey ahead of us."

Get Tools for Endurance

Because an emotional or physical condition may involve a lengthy process of recovery, it is important to have tools for endurance. If we do not know how to endure, we will simply succumb to discouragement and bitterness, ceasing to believe that healing is even possible. Since we do not know exactly when or how God will choose to intervene we must keep our hearts and minds ready to hear His word of correction or direction. It is harder to receive from His hand if we are focusing down on the problem rather than looking and reaching up to Him.

Watch Out for Discouraging Words from Others

It is important to be with people who have experienced God's healing power—they can communicate faith to us. By the same token, we need to watch out for those who have been defeated by their circumstances and expect others to be defeated also. In fact, some people would welcome another person's defeat because they want commiseration with their own experiences.

For example, when I experienced my two-year period of suffering, an individual who had experienced similar symptoms said, "I've had this condition off and on for years. You just have to work your life around the symptoms. They happen at the most inconvenient times. Last year the pain began again when I was on a trip, and then later just before my daughter's wedding. You just never know when your body will let you down!"

As I listened to her words, I felt my morale sinking. I envisioned episodes of pain coming at times when I knew I would need to be strong and healthy. I wondered, *Would this pain finally completely dominate my life?* My anxiety level rose as those frightening pictures played across my mind.

Proverbs 18:21 tells us that life and death are in the power of the tongue. When we indulge it, we shall eat its fruit. I knew that I could no longer afford to listen to words that promoted fear and discouragement. I had to have a plan.

First, I resolved to avoid discouraging people. I learned to identify conversations that would begin with sympathy, move quickly into unhealthy identification and end in discouragement. I learned to thank the individual for her concern, express my desire for her own recovery and withdraw politely from her company.

Second, I decided to apply 2 Corinthians 10:5 to overcome the anxiety-producing words and images in my mind. I practiced refuting every argument and reasoning "that sets itself up against the (true) knowledge of God." I learned to take every discouraging word to Scripture and exchange it for the truth.

For example, if a physician said, "I think you'd better just make up your mind to live with this pain," I would counter his statement with God's Word. I would apply Psalm 107:14, which says, "He brought them out of darkness and the shadow of death, and broke apart the bonds that held them," and verse 20, which says, "He sends forth His word and heals them and rescues them from the pit and destruction."

As I continued to combine God's Word and my healthy imagination, I was able to see my Father rescuing me. Peace would be established in my mind again.

Watch What You Say to Yourself

During one difficult period, if someone else did not discourage me I managed to discourage myself. In a conversation with a friend I heard myself saying, "I don't know if I'll ever get better. I don't think my doctor knows what he's doing. In fact, *he* admits that he doesn't know what to do next." Finally I just sighed, slumped down in my chair, folded my arms over my chest and concluded, "I just don't see how I'll ever make it through this." My friend looked at me and exclaimed, "Lynda, if you're not careful, you're going to talk yourself right out of your faith!"

I was astounded! I realized that my words had directly contradicted the Word of God. Not only were my words false and filling me with distress, they showed no respect for Jesus. I was disregarding His years of faithfulness to me. I asked His forgiveness, determining never to voice such faithless words again.

Remember That Nostalgia Is Not Your Friend

When suffering is prolonged it is easy to compare the current situation to a time when life seemed better and easier. Doing this, however, can make us resentful and angry. King Solomon warned us about making such comparisons when he said, "Do not say, Why were the old days better than these? For it is not wise or because of wisdom that you ask this" (Ecclesiastes 7:10).

A good biblical example of this is Job, for during his time of trial he fell into the trap of comparisons. He looked back upon his life and exclaimed,

> Oh, that I were as in the months of old, as in the days when God watched over me; when His lamp shone above and upon my head, and by His light I walked through darkness; . . . when the Almighty was yet with me, and my children were about me; when my steps [through rich pasturage] were washed with butter, and

the rock poured out for me streams of oil! When I went out to the gate of the city, when I prepared my seat in the street—the broad place [for the council at the city's gate]; the young men saw me, and hid themselves; the aged rose up and stood.

Job 29:2–8

Can you hear Job longing for the past seasons of success, prosperity and prestige? As his grief overwhelmed him, he began to justify himself, finding reasons why he did not deserve his trials.

In his despair, Job continued,

I delivered the poor who cried, the fatherless and him who had none to help him. The blessing of him who was about to perish came upon me, and I caused the widow's heart to sing for joy. I put on righteousness and it clothed me . . . my justice was like a robe . . . or a crown! I was eyes to the blind, and feet was I to the lame. I was a father to the poor and needy.

Job 29:12–16

Instead of keeping his mind on God's goodness, Job fixed his eyes on his own goodness and fell into self-righteousness. And it began with self-pity: "I am weary of my life and loathe it! I will give free expression to my complaint; I will speak in the bitterness of my soul" (10:1).

If we fail to remain vigilant regarding our attitudes, we will make the same mistake that Job did, believing that our own goodness exceeds the goodness of God. Then we may reject God as well as His help.

Watch What You See

Visual input is a powerful stimulus to the mind. If you are in a time of endurance, be very careful about what you let yourself see.

Betty, a friend who suffered from lupus, said, "When I first became sick, I was drawn to watch medical dramas on television. Perhaps I was hoping to find a clue to my own health. More often than not, though, those shows were filled with intense life-and-death moments, followed by death and sadness. Even if a program ended well, it was usually a bittersweet experience for me. When I watched a program before bedtime, the drama would invade my dreams."

Betty continued, "I decided that I was too emotionally vulnerable to watch programs that might provoke fear or sadness in my mind. I realized that I had been actually tempting myself to worry. I read Matthew 6:22, which says, 'The eye is the lamp of the body. So, if your eye is sound, your entire body will be full of light.' I stopped watching anything that caused me to feel shaken because I wanted my body to be full of light."

Reject Fear and Worry

Why do Christians worry about what may happen— or what did happen? For many of us, worry is almost a lifestyle. We do not even realize when we do it. I believe that we worry because we have deceived ourselves into believing that worry has value. For example, some of our deceptions are:

"Worry Is Progress"

Roberta, a chronic worrier, said, "If all I can do is worry about my condition, at least I *feel as if* I am doing something about it." Worry creates a false sense of progress, causing us to believe that we have actually made a valid contribution to our healing. The truth is that when we worry, we are wasting the energy that our body could use toward healing.

"Worry Will Protect Me"

Many believe that worry will magically prevent catastrophe. A man who was facing possible brain surgery said, "If I worry enough, maybe they won't find anything wrong."

Do you believe that worry will protect you? Have you deceived yourself in this way? Worry is a contradiction to faith and it cannot protect us. It can lead to an increase of illness.

A woman named Alice who was three months pregnant was diagnosed with breast cancer. She said, "I would rather worry about losing my breast than losing my baby." Believing that worry was her only choice, she chose to distract herself from the fear of losing her child by focusing on the loss of her breast instead. When we distract ourselves from worry about one thing by worrying about another, we lose opportunities to make a legitimate search for healing.

In addition, we can fall into the trap of obsessive-compulsive behavior. A client named Allie experienced this: "Buried memories of being sexually molested as a child began to flash into my mind, causing me to feel frightened and ashamed. I began doing something very strange. I noticed that the memories seemed to surface as I drove to work every morning. I would arrive at work feeling very shaken, unable to concentrate. So one day as I reached the first light past my house, I thought, *I wonder if I hit someone when I came out of my driveway?* I made myself drive back to check. Of course I found no body. Then I drove as far as the corner again and thought, *I wonder if I just overlooked the body? I'll go back and check.* Then I would drive back to my house, searching the area for the body of someone I might have hit. After being obsessed for weeks with the thought that I had hit someone while driving, I suddenly understood the reason for my behavior: As long as I continued those tormenting actions, not a single memory of sexual abuse had surfaced."

Allie managed to block all memories of sexual abuse by her repetitious, compulsive behaviors. At the same time, however, she became trapped in a tormenting obsessive pattern. In order for Allie to become well, she would have to allow the memories to surface. She had only succeeded in delaying her healing.

When we choose to worry our problems can become magnified. Are you a worrier? Have you allowed worry and fear to become your coping mechanisms? If so, are you willing to allow God to exchange your worry for faith? Faith will lighten your load and leave you free to explore advantages that will be truly productive for you.

Seek Guidance Continually for the Next Step

Kenn, a godly man who has suffered intensely for more than twenty-five years due to pain from a neck injury, said, "There are three things that I do every day. First, I pray that God will do whatever will bring Him the most glory. That is my prayer of surrender and abandonment to Him. Second, I ask God to speak, revealing anything He wants to tell me in the context of this affliction. Third, I ask God what He wants me to do next. I just ask Him for the next step."

As Kenn discovered, when we are suffering physically or emotionally it is easy to become overwhelmed. Our path becomes clearer when we simply look for the next step. When we follow through on that step, we can face the next one. Seeking guidance for one step at a time can prevent us from being overwhelmed.

Be Discerning About Physicians and Procedures

One of my clients named Jack told me: "I made the mistake of thinking that all doctors were equal. Now I've discovered that there are good doctors, and there are great doctors. I've also seen that there are very traditional doctors who tend to give up when well-established procedures do not bring results. Other doctors are more creative, inspired to search out and try new methods. I call these doctors Bird Dog Docs. A Bird Dog Doc is more likely to work with you as long as there is life left, always challenged to continue the search with new, innovative techniques."

Remember that the search for a medical cure can be a lengthy process. Explore all of your options before agreeing to any procedures. Ask questions. Go to the library or use the computer to get all the data you can about your condition. Do not depend on your doctor automatically to communicate all of your options. In addition to becoming responsible for getting information, make sure that you have the most qualified doctor to treat your particular condition. As I found, experience counts a lot.

If you are suffering emotionally, you may need to visit with several different counselors before you find one you can relate to easily. If you are going to pour out your heart, it is important to feel comfortable, relaxed and safe. Many who seek counseling make one appointment, and if that visit is not satisfactory they give up on counseling altogether.

Avoid Focusing on Statistics

Bill, my friend who suffered for a time from prostate cancer, learned the importance of not focusing on statistics. He says, "When I was first diagnosed, I asked the doctor what my chances were. As soon as I heard his answer, my morale plunged downward. His words resounded over and over in my ears for a few days. Then I decided that it was not he who had the last word, but God. Although I agreed to follow all of my doctor's instructions, I decided not to be influenced by statistics again. Instead I vowed to place my faith in the promises of God rather than in medical predictions or in the experiences of other people."

Avoid Isolation

When we do not feel good either physically or emotionally, it is tempting to withdraw, believing that we are not good company. We may even think that no one would want to be with us. If we withdraw, it becomes easy to succumb to self-pity because our avenues of encouragement are cut off. Then we are not only sick but also lonely and discouraged.

Ask for Help

A manager of a large corporation told me, "A man in our office killed himself. I have never been so surprised! No one realized he had any problems. He never missed work and he walked in with a smile every morning. He was a hard worker and he never caused trouble. After his death we discovered that his wife had left him a year ago. She had taken his infant son and simply disappeared. We had no idea. He had shut himself off from all of us."

There are times when we do not feel like asking someone for help, but those may be the times when we need to ask for help the most. Do not deprive yourself of help from those who know the Lord and would be glad to listen. It may be that their prayers will help bring the answer to your healing.

When I was sick it was difficult for me to ask for help. I had always been the one people came to for help. Now my role was reversed. As I resisted asking for help I realized that I had a problem with pride. As my pain became more constant, I did not want to admit that my faith was failing.

One day I called my pastor and said, "I am hurting so badly that my faith is hanging by a thread. I feel as if God has abandoned me. Will you call the elders to pray for me?" Not only did he call the elders, but he prayed with me often until I was well.

There are times when each of us needs help, and the sooner we humble ourselves the better. If you need help, it may be time to make the same decision that I did. Will you choose pride or help?

Let others help you. The blessing will be theirs as well as yours.

Never Think That It Is Too Late

If you have been suffering for a long time, you may be sinking into the belief that your condition is God's will. Do not stop praying and do not give up your search. It is never too late to get well. You may simply be on a plateau . . . or in a desert . . . but do not give up.

Nina suffered from TMJ, a painful joint dysfunction, for eight years. She related, "Years ago I began having tremendous pain in my jaw. I went to a dentist who told me that I needed to have a wisdom tooth pulled in order to adjust my bite. I did this, but I only became worse. Then he ground off most of my teeth, replacing them with crowns, hoping to make a better fit for my bite. After I had logged in hours in the dentist's chair, the pain increased even more. I was desperate and was afraid to let another doctor try to help me. However, I did eventually begin seeking help again, going from one doctor to another for years, experimenting with numerous treatments. I only experienced more pain and failure.

"One day as I was praying, I asked God to let me know if He wanted me ever to get well. I wondered if He wanted me to accept this condition as a thorn in the flesh. I had recently made a fresh commitment to Him, offering Him all that I am, and I had received a new desire to serve Him for the rest of my life. I was willing to keep my commitment even if the pain persisted. During that prayer time, the name of an old friend came to mind. My friend was a dentist who referred me to one final specialist out of state. I felt led of God to submit to the treatment that he recommended. After several months of reconstructive work, I was finally free of jaw pain! My life has been changed forever. I'm so glad I never gave up."

Do you think Nina would have been cured of TMJ if she had not continued to pursue healing? Do you believe that her total surrender played a part in her healing? Have you been tempted to resign yourself to suffering, resisting help? If you have, do what Nina did. Never give up.

A dear friend named Thomas had almost given up when he shared his secret story with me. He told me: "I was nine years old when a man molested me. Even though I tried to keep that memory out of my mind, it continued to torment me. It affected the way I treated my wife and children. It damaged my sense of self-worth."

After Thomas told me his story, I began to pray for him, asking God to give him freedom from the shame and disgrace he felt. Several months passed. Nothing happened, but I continued to pray.

One day Thomas called me and told me an astonishing conclusion to his story: "I was working in my store when I looked up and saw the man who had molested me! He was crossing the street in front of my store. I recognized him immediately even after all these years. He came right into my store and began making a sales pitch. Anger and desire for revenge overcame me and I asked him to walk outside for a moment. He followed me to a deserted area of the parking lot where I proceeded to hit him, knocking him to the ground. As he lay there grasping his abdomen, he looked up and asked, 'Why are you doing this to me?' I told him that the beating he had just received was from the nine-year-old boy he had molested years ago."

Thomas told me that the man began to weep, pleading for forgiveness. As the man knelt on the ground, he cried, "I've been in therapy for years because of the guilt and shame I felt for what I did to you. I have prayed for the opportunity to ask your forgiveness. Could you ever find it in your heart to forgive me?"

Thomas forgave the man, offering him the opportunity to receive release. Thomas concluded, "I forgave him. As I walked back into my store, I knew I was a healed man, totally released from all those years of shame."

Only God could have arranged for the timely meeting of those two grown men who lived in different states. I was amazed at the way God not only presented a way for Thomas to be healed but provided release for the perpetrator as well.

Ecclesiastes 3:1 tells us that there is a time for every matter and purpose and a time for every good work. We may never understand why some healing takes so long, but we must not let the length of time convince us that it is not God's will for us to be released and healed.

As long as there is life, prayers for healing can be answered. A man named John told me of an answer to a prayer his mother had prayed for fifty years.

"My father died when my mother was thirty-four years old, so she raised my brother and me alone," he said. "During my teenage years, I rebelled against the faith my mother had instilled in me. I disregarded her love and admonitions for about seven years. I knew that my attitude and actions broke my mother's heart."

He continued, "I grew up, went to medical school, and eventually embraced the faith of my childhood again. I informed my mother of my decision, and although she was happy I sensed that something was missing.

"Years later my mother told my wife that she really needed me to ask her forgiveness for the years of heartbreak I had caused her. Even when my wife told me of my mother's need, I did not comply.

"Eventually my mother developed Alzheimer's disease, which robbed her of all her faculties. As she neared her final days on earth, I shared with a small group my regret that I had not asked her forgiveness, commenting that it was too late because she could no longer comprehend my words. At that stage of her illness my mother appeared unreachable. She had not spoken in months. She could not feed herself and she was incontinent. Often she would cry like a lost child."

John continued, "As I told my story to the group, I got in touch with my mother's need for the first time. Regardless of her condition, I decided to apologize to her for the hurt I had caused. Visiting her, I knelt down before her chair, looked her right in the eye and expressed my contrition and grief. The most amazing thing happened! As she looked at me, her expression cleared and for the first time in months, she actually spoke! She looked directly at me and replied, 'It's all right, John.' Her caregivers and I were absolutely amazed. We knew that our moment of communication and clarity were gifts to us both. God had provided a time for my mother's broken heart to be healed before it was too late."

John concluded, "I believe that the Holy Spirit communicated my desire for forgiveness to my mother and enabled her to respond to me. Both of us were healed."

Do not ever minimize God's concerns for our needs because of timing. He always remembers our requests.

Engage in the Process of Personal Change

When I was sick I heard a woman say, "I choose to embrace my illness." Because I did not want to remain in pain, I did not choose to have the same attitude. However, I was aware that pain could be a great teacher as well as the doorway to many internal changes. Pain can bring us face-to-face with the fact that we are dependent upon God for every blessing . . . even the air we breathe. While you are waiting, look for the lessons God may want to teach you. Listen carefully. It may be a long time before you are as sensitized to your need for God as you are now. Even if you are still suffering physical or emotional pain, you will be rewarded by the personal changes you make.

A doctor friend told me, "I've seen more healthy spiritual transactions take place between God and my patients when my patients are flat on their backs in a hospital bed. Enforced stillness can place us in a strategic place to hear God." Even though it is not healthy to desire affliction, it is important to remember that healing can take place on many levels. Stay open to whatever God may want to do inside you.

Pour Out Your Heart to God

When tragedies occur or problems multiply, it is easy to forget that God truly is in control of our lives. Job felt this way when he said, "It profits a man nothing that he should delight himself with God and consent to Him" (Job 34:9). Job had momentarily decided that even God did not have the desire or ability to help him.

Be honest and forthright when you talk with God and He will be honest and forthright with you, engaging in dialogue with you. God's response to Job was, "Will you condemn Me [your God] that you may [appear] righteous and justified?" (Job 40:8). God engaged in personal confrontation with Job, reminding him that He is the One who is righteous and that He sets the boundaries around our lives. He reminded Job of His goodness as well as the fact that He has been in control from the beginning. When Job heard God's response, he said,

> [You said to me] who is this that darkens and obscures counsel [by words] without knowledge? Therefore [I now see] I have [rashly] uttered what I did not understand, things too wonderful for me, which I did not know. . . . I had heard of You [only] by the hearing of the ear; but now my [spiritual] eye sees you. Therefore I loathe [my words] and abhor myself, and repent in dust and ashes.
>
> JOB 42:3–6

When God's conversation with Job was over, the rift between them no longer existed.

Pray Without Ceasing

If your symptoms do not improve the first time you pray, do not assume that it is not God's will for you to be whole. Do not be ashamed to continue requesting prayer from those who care about you.

Doris, a radiant, healthy woman, told her story. "I had been through a long period of trauma. My husband left me and then my mother died. I had just moved into a new home and begun to feel comfortable there. Exterminators came to spray for termites one day, and when I came home from work I noticed a strong chemical smell. Because I was tired, I went to bed early. When I awoke the next morning I was unable to coordinate my brain with my hands. I could not find my way out of bed and I could not figure out how to dial my telephone. A neighbor finally came over to check on me, finding me disabled.

"After a long series of medical tests, I was told that my immune system had been damaged by the toxic chemicals in my home. There was no known treatment for me.

"After a period of shock and grief, I faced the necessity of moving out of my house. I had to sell all of my contaminated belongings. I slept outside until I could renovate another house with preservative-free materials. I became allergic to everything I ate, touched, smelled or wore. I had rashes, itching, respiratory problems, headaches and stomach problems. Even my bones ached. I felt as if my life was over.

"Because I was so aware of the fragility of my immune system, I became afraid to go out of my house or office. Fear became my primary disease, even more crippling than the effects of the toxic substances.

"I received some counseling and asked regularly for healing prayer. Over a period of several years, my fears and my symptoms completely ceased! Today I am able to do whatever I choose, go wherever I want to go. In fact, during the last few years I have toured France, Italy, Germany, Turkey, Mexico, Canada, England, Switzerland, Jamaica and Alaska. I have stayed in all types of accommodations. I have eaten food in all of those countries without having any difficulties. I am blessed in every area of my life. I can hardly remember what it was like to be sick."

The healing prayers that Doris received sustained her through periods of fear and doubt, giving her immune system time to gain strength from week to week. Doris concluded, "That was a dreadful experience, but I did draw very close to God during that time. I know that I would not have recovered without His healing power and sustaining grace. Without the constant prayers of people, I would not have been able to hang on until my recovery was complete."

Faith and Patience

I want to share one more story with you on the importance of endurance in the often long walk of healing. A friend named Gay learned lessons about faith and patience that carried her through many long months of treatment. I hope that her story will encourage you, too.

Gay's Story

As a little girl, I believed in Jesus, but as I grew up, I seemed to "outgrow" Him. I felt that I should handle life's difficulties by myself and for years I did rather well.

As I grew older, my battles became more difficult and costly, but I still insisted on going my own way. I pursued knowledge from all the self-help books that came along. I finally obtained a master's degree in counseling. I thought, *Now I'm a therapist! I should be able to handle my problems.* I had earned the tools to do that job.

I struggled through my thirties and forties with two failed marriages and had recently married for the third time. I had also discovered that my father had adopted me. I set about the task of meeting my biological father. Then my mother passed away. Stress was at a high level in my life. Three years later I was diagnosed with ovarian cancer. I was devastated. This was no job for a therapist! I needed a miracle and I needed God.

I bought every book and tape on healing I could find. I determined to become the exceptional patient. As usual, I was going to take this trip alone and under my own power.

From the first, however, I began to notice that God showed up in a big way. I had gone to the doctor for a distended abdomen. It was diagnosed as a dietary problem. The next day, when I told a friend about my diagnosis she excused herself to make a phone call. When she returned, she informed me that she had made an emergency appointment for me with an OB-GYN. One hour later, I was told that I needed a biopsy immediately. I was alone and scared.

Immediately I called my husband, Jim, who is a pilot and was told that he had already taxied out of the hangar and was awaiting the signal to take off. Just by chance he called back to the hangar on the company radio. His action was very unusual, but it enabled him to learn of my condition. He turned the plane around, returned to the hangar and was replaced by another crewman. Jim was able to be with me at the time of the biopsy. I was grateful that God sent Jim back so that I would not be alone.

On the next Monday we were informed that I had cancer, and the surgery was already scheduled for the next day. I met with the surgeon that afternoon and just didn't feel right about it. Later that day, I got a call from a friend who said, "Do yourself a favor and check out the hospital in Zion, Illinois. They have a holistic approach to cancer that not only includes medicine, but nutrition, spirituality and psychoneuroimmunology." Well, that was a match for me. I canceled my plans for surgery and made plans to go to Zion. I believed that God again had intervened to direct me.

That evening God sent another friend by with healing Scripture tapes from his church. He explained God's desire to heal me and invited me to a prayer service, a women's Bible study on healing, as well as to a home group of believers that would assist our entire family. All of a sudden I felt a surge of real hope.

As we left for Zion, I thought about a recurring dream I had had for several months. In my dream, a very tall man would come to me and say, "Everything is going to be all right." I had never discussed the dream with anyone until I got to the hospital at Zion. While

I was sitting in the lobby of the hospital, a six-foot-five man came whistling through the door. I called out, "I'm so glad to see a happy person!" He came over and introduced himself as the pastor of the hospital. I knew instantly who he was! He was the man in my dream. I experienced an even deeper level of peace.

My surgery and treatment began on the following Monday. I had a Christian doctor as well as a pastor. I was equipped with my healing tapes, and a wonderful group of believers prayed for me.

I went into remission quickly, but chose to do a stem cell replacement procedure. It was an added insurance against the return of cancer. I did well with the procedure and was released in record time. I played my healing tapes continually and even slept with my Bible beside me.

My treatment was finished six months later, and I used the next four months to recover. However, when I went back for a checkup, I was diagnosed with a recurrence. My family and I were devastated again. At that point, my faith began to weaken. I realized how much a bad medical report could shake my faith. I asked the doctors not to give me any more statistics or reports. It's hard to build your house in a storm, but it's not impossible if you protect yourself from unnecessary strain.

I would hear and read reports of how God had healed people more quickly than He was healing me. I would find their healings encouraging, but at the same time I would wonder, *Why not me, God? Where's my miracle? How long am I going to have to wait? What are they doing that I'm not doing? Do they have more faith than I do? Do I need to get more people to pray?* I began to take the burden of my healing upon myself. I soon realized that I could make myself crazy with doubt and confusion. I also heard about people who died from cancer.

It was during this time that I began to learn about faith and patience. I learned that patience is not just a nice personality trait, but an overcoming force that could keep me going day to day. Patience will gird up your faith when you feel weak. When situations are dark, we can easily become overwhelmed. I would repeat Psalm 30:5 to myself: "Weeping may endure for a night, but joy comes in the morning." I had to learn to yield to patience.

James 1:4 in the King James Version says, "Let patience have her perfect work." I learned that patience would cause me to go home, climb back into bed and listen to my healing tapes or read God's Word. Victory comes when we simply persist in doing what we already know to do. When I found myself struggling in faith, it helped me to know that it was not my faith that was weak, but it was my patience that needed to be released. Faith and patience are two separate forces and each plays a separate role.

Faith is developed by the Word of God. Patience comes as we agree to walk through the story and stop demanding a quick resolution.

I memorized the King James Version of Romans 5:1–4, which says, "Therefore being justified by faith, we have peace with God through our Lord Jesus Christ: . . . And not only so, but we glory in tribulations also: knowing that tribulation worketh patience; and patience, experience; and experience, hope."

I continued to live my life like a normal person as much as possible. My children received Christ, and we began to fight as a family. My husband and children never treated me as though I had "cancer" as a noun, but more like an adjective.

We never stopped doing things or planning our future. We all went on a ski trip to Tahoe, and I skied all day every day. My doctors were amazed when I told them that I didn't need statistics about the probability of my recovery. I had decided to believe the prognosis of Jehovah Rapha. That works for me.

Although Gay chose the treatment approach that she felt was best for her, there are numerous treatments for cancer, and I suggest that you become well-informed and discuss every option with your doctor. Nevertheless, faith and patience enabled Gay to walk on level ground spiritually and emotionally, bringing her, as well as others, closer to Jesus.

Although we are promised trials in this life, God never allows our trials to damage us beyond His ability to bring good to us and glory to Himself. Stay close to Him. Be willing to do all that is required. Follow step-by-step. Nothing that comes our way is without purpose or possibility.

Suggested Prayer

Father, do not allow me to lose heart and give up. When I am weary, please come to my aid. When I lack faith, help my unbelief. Please bring Your words of encouragement back to my mind and lift me up.

Please lead me to physicians who can help me and provide medications that I may need. Sustain me through all procedures and treatment that may be required. Holy Spirit, always be at work in me. Let me be confident that You are always with me, leading me in the ways I need to go.

Father, give me an undivided heart. You know where my doubts and confusion lie. Please teach me truth and give me clarity.

Lord, cause me to humble myself to receive help from others. Forgive me for complaining. Enable me to discipline myself to apply Your Word continually to my mind and help me to be patient in my journey. Create in me the desire to honor You in all that I say or do, remembering that You are always on my side.

Father, cause me to love You more each day. In Jesus' name, I receive Your healing power into my being and bless You. Amen.

Avenues to Healing

God has given us many avenues by which we may experience healing. These avenues, given by example throughout the Bible, show us His love and availability. Through them we may experience His Presence as our Healer.

The Laying On of Hands

Often when Jesus prayed for people, He reached out and touched them (see Mark 6:5; 7:32–35; 16:18; Luke 4:40; 13:13). When He laid His hands on them, they were released from their afflictions. His touch transmitted the healing power of His Father to their minds, spirits and bodies. It also communicated His compassion for their suffering.

Jesus also instructed His disciples to lay hands on people who needed help. Mark 16:17–18 says: "And these attesting signs will accompany those who believe: . . . they will lay their hands on the sick, and they will get well." Jesus assured believers that even though He would ascend into heaven, He would always work in and through them here on earth. His power would always accompany their actions. Mark 16:20 tells us that "they went out and preached everywhere, while the Lord kept working with them and confirming the message by the attesting signs and miracles." When our Father asks us to minister in Jesus' name, He promises to send His power to do the work. As believers, we need to be ready to touch people and open the way.

A woman named Junanne, who had suffered terribly from food allergies, was healed when hands were laid upon her during a prayer time with friends. She said, "I had been sick most of the time since I was eight years old. My condition appeared to be genetic in origin."

Due to allergies, as well as poor eating habits during high school, Junanne became very ill by the time she entered early adulthood. "In fact," she said, "it was my ill health that caused me to see my need for God. I gave my life to Christ, and for several years my health improved."

Then her family moved to a different state where the climate was hot and damp and she began to feel an onslaught of allergens upon her system again. She became as sick as she had been in her early twenties, unable to function on many days.

"I had to pace myself all the time," she told me. "If I needed to buy groceries and go to the cleaners, I would have to choose which errand I would run first. Then I would have to go home and lie down before I could take care of the next item on my list. My ears hurt constantly, and I was always extremely fatigued."

Being the mother of two small children, Junanne's illness was a tremendous handicap. One day, observing the torment of her illness, some friends asked her if she had ever prayed for healing.

Junanne continued: "I had to admit that I had not asked God to heal me. I knew that my illness had brought me to God, and that it reminded me constantly of my need to depend upon Him. I guess I had assumed that, because my illness had been useful in some ways, God intended to use it to that effect for the rest of my life."

Junanne told me that after her friends laid hands on her and prayed for healing, she had absolutely no symptoms for several days. Then the symptoms started once more and her friends laid hands upon her and prayed again; she experienced relief immediately. When the symptoms returned after a few days, she requested prayer again, and this time her symptoms did not return.

Junanne concluded: "There was a bonus healing for our family at this point, too. Our eight-year-old son had inherited the same allergies that I had, and after the third time of prayer he was also healed! We have been able to eat like normal people for months."

Once a man asked, "Why is it necessary for someone to lay hands on me? Why isn't it just as effective simply to say a prayer?" Studies have shown that touch is comforting to those who are suffering. Touch also provides a physical reminder that God is very near, that His healing power is available. Regardless of the practical reasons, we should follow the instructions of Jesus.

Anointing with Oil

In the Old Testament we read that kings, priests and prophets were anointed with oil upon being commissioned into service. Oil is a symbol of the power of the Holy Spirit; thus, each recipient was equipped by this act to meet the requirements of his office. In the New Testament we are instructed to anoint the sick with oil. James 5:14–15 tells us that when we pray the prayer of faith as we anoint the sick, the Lord will save, restore and forgive. God offers a visible, concrete way for those who hurt to become aware of His availability and power. Anointing with oil is a visible action that illustrates an invisible transaction: the healing power of God upon the body of a human being. Other rituals that provide a visible illustration of an inner transaction are water baptisms, weddings and funerals.

Bonnie suffered for years with severe allergies, headaches and sinus infections. She took allergy injections four days a week for several years, but the medication did not cure her. One day she attended a healing service at her church. When she knelt at the altar for prayer the priest anointed her with oil, applying the oil in the shape of a cross on her forehead. Immediately, her thoughts turned to the cross and the blood of Christ. A feeling of intense warmth began to penetrate her skin where the priest had placed the oil. In fact, Bonnie told me she retained the feeling of warmth on her forehead for hours after she left the church. Several days later, she realized that all of her allergy symptoms had ceased. More than twenty years have passed, and Bonnie has never had another allergy shot. She told me, "I have never forgotten the sacredness of the moment when the priest anointed me with oil. I felt so near to God."

Deliverance and Spiritual Warfare

Several instances in Scripture give account of illnesses directly caused by Satan. The gospel of Luke tells of a woman who "for eighteen years had had an infirmity caused by a spirit [a demon of sickness]. She was bent completely forward and utterly unable to straighten herself or to look upward. . . . Then He laid [His] hands on her and instantly she was made straight" (Luke 13:11–13). Paul attributes his "thorn" or painful affliction to a messenger from Satan (2 Corinthians 12:7). Satan is also the one who afflicts Job (Job 1:11–12). He is an aggressive enemy.

In my work I occasionally encounter those who are bound by ungodly thoughts and behaviors. Some have sexual addictions; others are addicted to substances. Many are afflicted with fears, depression, obsessions and self-condemnation. When I meet a person who cannot control his thoughts or actions, I ask, "Is this really *you*? Is this what you really want, or do you simply feel pressured to do it?"

I ask that question because Satan has the ability to tempt us, to make us weak and to bind us to evil. Recently a man named Brandon told me: "I feel so weak. No matter how hard I try, I fail. I seem to have lost all self-control. I give in to my impulses and afterward, I feel so guilty. Then shame takes over. It's a cycle. It happens over and over. What is happening to me?"

If you are a believer experiencing repeated failure and torment, you may be asking the same question, "What is happening to me?"

Jesus knows what is happening. In John 10:10 He explains: "The thief comes only in order that he may steal and may kill and may destroy. I came that they may have and enjoy life, and have it in abundance—to the full, till it overflows." Jesus gives us a perfect contrast between His purposes and those of Satan.

Throughout the gospels we read how Jesus confronted Satan's evil agents, defeating them and setting people like Brandon free. Mark 1:32–34, for example, says this: "Now when it was evening, after the sun had set, they brought to Him all who were sick and those under the power of demons, until the whole town was gathered together about the door. And He cured many who were afflicted with various diseases, and He drove out many demons."

Jesus knew that the disciples would encounter the same situations in their ministries, so He instructed them: "Cure the sick; raise the dead; cleanse the lepers; drive out demons" (Matthew 10:8). Because Jesus also knew the torment that evil spirits can inflict upon us,

His parting words before ascending into heaven were: "And these attesting signs will accompany those who believe: in My name they will drive out demons" (Mark 16:17).

After Pentecost, when the disciples were filled with the Holy Spirit, they continued to set people free by the authority of Jesus' name. Acts 5:16 says: "And the people gathered also from the towns and hamlets around Jerusalem, bringing the sick and those troubled with foul spirits, and they were all cured." Jesus did not leave us without a way to escape our bondage and torment. He left us the authority of His name and sent us His power. In Acts 16:18 we see the account of the slave girl who was possessed by a spirit of divination. Paul turned to her and said to the spirit within her, "I charge you in the name of Jesus Christ to come out of her!" And we are told that the spirit left her that very moment.

Greg, a tall young pastor with black hair, leaned forward earnestly as he began to tell me how he was delivered from the bondage of Satan. Tears formed in his eyes as he recalled the torment of previous years. "Although my father was a pastor, I rebelled during my adolescence. My relationship with my family became very strained when I began to use drugs and moved in with my girlfriend. For several years my life spiraled downward. I became full of fear and deceit, involved in witchcraft and sexual immorality. I refused to recognize that the emotional torment and confusion I was experiencing was the result of my behavior.

"When I reached college age, I came to my senses and returned to my faith. However, I was unable to separate myself mentally and emotionally from the past. I became very intimidated by the forces of darkness, which still bound me, but I avoided any opportunity to receive release.

"I volunteered to go on a mission trip to England one summer. On that trip, I found myself in a congregation of believers who actually prayed for people to be set free from demonic bondage. I knew that, even though I was a believer in Christ, I was oppressed in many areas of my mind. There were times when fear dominated my thoughts and controlled my life. I was continually tormented with temptation to return to my old ways of living.

"God brought me face-to-face with an elderly woman in her eighties. She was tiny and soft-spoken, but mighty in spirit. As we sat down together I told her of my past, expressing my desire for complete deliverance.

"This precious woman of Christ asked me to stand with her for prayer. She simply placed her hand on my chest and said, 'Precious Jesus, set him free.' At that moment, the power of God came upon me and I found myself on my knees, kneeling on the floor. As my friend knelt beside me, commanding unclean spirits to leave me, I felt warfare going on inside my body as well as my soul. Satanic darts were thrown at my mind and I thought, 'This isn't going to work. There is no help for me.' I immediately told my friend that I needed help with fear and unbelief. As she continued to pray over me, I was finally released. I felt the dark heaviness lift off of me. Suddenly it seemed as if the oil of the Holy Spirit began to flow onto me, penetrating my entire being.

"As I walked home that night, in my mind's eye, I could see myself clothed in my spiritual armor. I sensed such a pure, raw sense of power. All fear of the demonic was gone, because I had witnessed personally the overcoming power of the Holy Spirit to deliver me. It was after that deliverance prayer that I really was able to begin a close walk with the Lord."

As Greg's experience illustrates, evil spirits may be allowed to afflict people mentally and physically, but their power is limited. When Satan afflicted Job, for example, God limited his power: "Behold he is in your hand; only spare his life." God sets the limits and He enables us to overcome.

First Peter 5:8–9 gives us a protection plan:

Be well-balanced—temperate, sober-minded; be vigilant and cautious at all times, for that enemy of yours, the devil, roams around like a lion roaring [in fierce hunger], seeking someone to seize upon and devour. Withstand him; be firm in faith [against his onset],—rooted, established, strong, immovable and determined—knowing that the same (identical) sufferings are appointed to your brotherhood (the whole body of Christians) throughout the world.

You may be asking the question, Can a Christian be possessed by an evil spirit? A Christian cannot be *possessed* as in *ownership* because a believer who has been born again by the blood of Jesus Christ is "stamped with the seal of the long-promised Holy Spirit" (Ephesians 1:13) and cannot be possessed by a spirit of Satan. The Holy Spirit is our Father's eternal seal of ownership upon us, bought by Jesus on the cross. Even though we cannot be possessed, however, we can become *oppressed* by evil spirits. To *oppress* means "to lie heavily on the mind or to weigh down." Oppression brings a sensation of heaviness and darkness. Satan can torment believers, but he cannot own them.

As God delivered Greg from the effects of the evil one, so He wants to deliver all of His children from evil afflictions. Every believer has the right to take up the authority of the name of Jesus Christ when Satan comes to torment (see Philippians 2:9–10). Ask God to give you the ability to recognize the subtle approach of the evil one. If you believe you are being oppressed, recognize that you cannot free yourself. Confess your complete dependence upon God. Repent of any sins that may have opened the door to your affliction. Ask to be forgiven and cleansed. As you begin to pray, thank God for His presence with you. Pray to be filled with the Holy Spirit. In the name of Jesus Christ, refuse Satan and begin to praise God for His great power to deliver you. If you are experiencing an emotional or physical affliction that has not responded to traditional treat-

ask about this

ment, ask for spiritual discernment concerning your condition. If you feel that you need assistance with prayer, ask someone who understands the delivering power of God to pray with you.

Always remember one of the primary reasons God sent Jesus into the world: "The reason the Son of God was made manifest (visible) was to undo (destroy, loosen and dissolve) the works the devil [has done]" (1 John 3:8).

Communion

You may wonder what Communion has to do with healing. Under the Old Covenant, God's people were granted blessings as they met the requirements of the Law. One of the blessings God promised to give them was healing. For example, Deuteronomy 7:12, 15 says:

> And if you hearken to these precepts and keep and do them, the Lord your God will keep with you the covenant and the steadfast love which He swore to your fathers. . . . And the Lord will take away from you all sickness, and none of the evil diseases of Egypt, which you knew, will He put upon you, but will lay them upon all who hate you.

When Jesus shed His blood for us on the cross, He established a New Covenant, one in which believers may receive blessings by faith, according to God's grace. First Peter 2:24 tells us: "He personally bore our sins in His [own] body to the tree [as to an altar and offered Himself on it], that we might die (cease to exist) to sin and live to righteousness. By His wounds you have been healed."

Because of Jesus' sacrifice, we no longer live under the Law. As we take the bread and the wine, we remember and give thanks for the grace that Jesus purchased for us from the cross.

I read the account of the crucifixion again recently, and I became more aware of the concrete physical evidence of power that was released when Jesus died. For example, the heavy curtain in the Temple was cut in two from top to bottom as if a well-targeted laser beam from heaven sliced it open. The power that was released made the earth shake so hard that rocks broke. Graves opened and people got up and walked into town!

Even though the earth does not shake every day and people do not come out of their graves and walk away from cemeteries, the power is still available to us. The same power that broke open a rock can change a heart. The same power that raised people from their graves can heal our bodies, deliver our minds and give us new life.

Three days after the crucifixion, God sent another dynamic display of power and raised Jesus from the dead. Pentecost soon followed and the Holy Spirit was poured out on all believers (see Acts 2:1–4). Romans 8:11 says that the same Spirit who raised Jesus from the dead lives inside our mortal bodies. What power was released from heaven at the cross! We truly have reason to remember and give thanks.

Debbie, suffering from multiple sclerosis, told me of the blessing she received through Communion. "Two years ago I was diagnosed with MS," she said. "My husband and I were terrified. As we waited for our final visit with the doctor, my husband began to cry and said, 'You can't have this. I've got to have you with me!' I was heartbroken at the thought of not being able to raise my children.

"We called the elders of our church to anoint me with oil and pray for me, and I began treatment. God sustained me through that year and I was able to continue to teach school, as well as care for my family. The next summer our family went to Destin, Florida, and while we were there we attended St. Andrews-by-the-Sea, an Episcopal church. We had heard that many people were healed of sickness as they went forward to receive Communion and healing prayer.

"I felt the Lord's presence clearly as I went to the altar and knelt for prayer. After I received the bread and wine, one of the elders knelt beside me, anointed my head with oil and prayed for me. I felt peace flood over me, and then I was amazed as I felt an energy come over my body like an electrical force. Later that day I went to walk on the beach. I had so much strength and felt so good that I turned cartwheels! Two years before that day, I could not even walk. I still have some symptoms of MS, but I am able to fulfill most of my daily responsibilities. I still recall the power of God that touched me that Sunday, and as I reflect on that experience, my faith and hope are sustained."

The Name of Jesus

The name of Jesus is the cornerstone of prayer. Philippians 2:9–10 tells us that the name of Jesus is above every name, and that every knee in heaven and earth must bow to that name.

Jesus told His disciples to ask for whatever they wanted in His name (see John 16:23). In Acts 4, John and Peter were questioned: "By what sort of power or by what kind of authority did [such people as] you do this [healing]?" Peter replied, "Let it be known and understood by you all, and by the whole house of Israel, that *in the name and through the power and authority of Jesus Christ* of Nazareth, Whom you crucified, [but] Whom God raised from the dead, in Him and by means [of Him] this man is standing here before you well and sound in body" (verses 7 and 10, emphasis added).

After Jesus' resurrection the disciples witnessed this healing, delivering power in His name. One day at the Temple they encountered a beggar who had been crippled from birth. When the man saw Peter and John, he asked them for a gift. Peter replied, "Silver and gold [money], I have none; but what I do have, that I give to you: in (the use of) the name of Jesus Christ of Nazareth, walk!" (Acts 3:6). When Peter took hold of the man's right hand and raised him to his feet, his legs immediately became strong and steady. He began to leap around the gate to the Temple as he praised God.

As the people watched in astonishment, Peter looked at them and said, "Why are you so surprised and wondering at this? Why do you keep staring at us, as though by our [own individual] power or [active] piety we had made [this man able] to walk? The God of Abraham and of Isaac and of Jacob, the God of our forefathers, has glorified His Servant and Son Jesus" (verses 12–13).

Peter realized that, although he had no power within his own humanity, there was all power in the name of Jesus. As believers in the Body of Christ, we have been given the same privilege of using the name of Jesus Christ to overcome all kinds of suffering.

Recently I was privileged to meet Gene, a man who received a miraculous healing when the name of Jesus was spoken on his behalf. Now at age 67, white-haired and still strong, he told me of a time when he had had no hope.

"I was in my mid-twenties," he began. "Because of a growth in my chest, surgeons had removed my right lung. They had to take three ribs with it, and they left an ugly hole in my back to provide drainage. That radical surgery left me with a drooping shoulder. In spite of their efforts, the bleeding continued. I suffered constant pain. I could not work and provide for my wife and two small children. I felt as though my life was over."

Gene was seldom able to leave his house, but one day when he did he saw a huge tent with a sign in front that proclaimed: "THE BLIND SEE! THE DEAF HEAR! THE LAME WALK!" A tent revival had come to Little Rock.

Gene said, "I was very skeptical, but I was also desperate." He visited with the evangelist who asked him what he wanted from God. Gene unbuttoned his shirt and showed the evangelist his scar. "I told him that I was missing three ribs and my right lung, my shoulder drooped, and I wanted every bit of it restored." Gene agreed to attend the next service and receive prayer.

Gene and his wife, Nancy, went to the huge tent that night. After the sermon, Gene joined the line of people who wanted to receive healing prayers. As Gene waited in line, a miracle occurred that wiped out his skepticism.

"I was standing right behind a man who was holding a baby with an ugly growth on his lip about the size of a dime" he said. "When the baby received prayer, that growth disappeared right before my eyes. I knew the power of God was really there."

Then it was Gene's turn in the healing line. "The evangelist didn't pray for me, but he told the congregation about my condition and asked them to extend their hands toward me and pray. I raised my hands to God.

"At that moment," Gene said, "I felt as if someone behind me had poured something very warm and thick over me. I turned around to see who had done it, but no one was there. Then suddenly I felt as though someone had blown up my chest. I knew God had healed me."

Gene's prayer was answered: His right lung and three ribs were instantly restored, the drainage hole in his back disappeared and his shoulder straightened up!

The next Monday Gene returned to work. The surgeon who had operated on him took numerous x-rays of his chest over a period of months to document the healing. His records were on file at Baptist Hospital. Gene told his story on a national television program and several newspapers carried the account of the miracle he received.

When I asked Gene how his healing had changed his life, he said, "It created a deep hunger in me to know

Jesus more deeply. I could not learn God's Word fast enough. I still feel the same way today. Jesus is my life."

As I listened to Gene's story, I remembered Jeremiah 33:3: "Call to Me and I will answer you and show you great and mighty things, fenced in and hidden, which you do not know—do not distinguish and recognize, have knowledge of and understand."

The Prayer of Faith

Dr. Terrance Zuerlein told me another account of a supernatural answer to prayer that he observed in his practice as a neonatal specialist. With excitement and joy, he stated: "Throughout my fourteen years as a physician in Newborn Intensive Care, I have always watched expectantly for those times in which the Lord God, Jehovah Rapha, would work mightily. I have personally witnessed multiple episodes in which God intervened supernaturally to heal in response to prayer. I have seen the all-knowing, self-sufficient and at times arrogant tongues of scientific medical knowledge turn silent upon witnessing that which they cannot explain. I saw this occur following the delivery of twins."

Dr. Zuerlein continued: "I was on call to cover high-risk deliveries on the day that J. N.'s mother delivered, having followed her in the high risk obstetrics clinic for several months. The twin infants in her womb were most likely identical and were sharing nutrition and oxygen flow from side-by-side placentas connected by unusual vessels. These vessels allowed J. N.'s twin to 'steal' nutrition from him, growing larger at J. N.'s expense. This phenomena is known as 'Twin-to-Twin Syndrome.' The twins were delivered by Caesarean section at the twenty-seventh week of pregnancy and both were critically ill as anticipated. J. N. weighed one pound six ounces, and his twin weighed four pounds. As is so often the case in this scenario, the larger twin was the sicker of the two. Both infants were on the ventilator respiratory support, antibiotics, intravenous fluids and cardiac support. J. N.'s twin was in florid congestive heart failure due to his 'stealing' blood away from J. N. In spite of our best efforts, J. N.'s twin died. Tears flowed as I gave the sad news to his parents.

"J. N. was now the surviving twin, and the eyes of his family and physician were upon him. Throughout the day his condition seemed to stabilize until five in the afternoon when it became evident that he had collapsed one of his lungs. A chest tube was placed and his lungs reinflated. Shortly thereafter, he began hemorrhaging from his intestinal tract. His respiratory status deteriorated, his blood pressure plummeted and he began to have acid accumulation in his bloodstream. The blood flowed out of his tiny fragile body as fast as I was transfusing it in. He began to hemorrhage from his breathing tube and all of his IV's.

"J. N. had only one chance for survival. He needed to be operated on immediately to repair the perforation and remove dead intestinal tissue. I called several pediatric surgeons as the night wore on, but all declined—speaking of the almost certain likelihood that he would die during surgery.

"When I went to J. N.'s parents at one in the morning, I offered to allow them to come and hold him before he died. J.N.'s father asked if he could call their pastor and elders to come and pray over J. N. He expressed his regret that he had not done this with his other son. When I told the night nurses that a group would be coming to pray for J. N., I was reminded that this was highly unusual, but I assured the nursery staff that I would take responsibility for the visit.

"By approximately two in the morning, eight men had assembled around J. N.'s warmer table. A season of fervent prayers of faith began as we locked arms around the tiny infant who was bleeding to death. We wept as we entreated God to spare the life of this small fragile representative of God's creation. I sensed the Holy Spirit in our midst as our prayer time came to an end. Then, 'inexplicably' the hemorrhage from J. N.'s intestine ceased! It had only been minutes since the group had left. His blood pressure and respiratory status improved and his urine output came back. By sunrise, his status had improved dramatically and I found a surgeon to repair the perforation. His condition continued to improve, and he came off the respirator and began feeding. After a long course of hospitalization, he went home to join his parents and siblings. When I saw him at age five, he was experiencing a little hearing loss, but he was a healthy and happy child. I witnessed a dramatic supernatural healing in answer to our prayers. I saw skeptics speak of the intense love of the believers who had prayed."

You may be thinking that a great deal of faith is required to receive an answered prayer like Dr. Zuerlein's. In Luke 17:5–6 the disciples expressed the same thought: "Increase our faith." Jesus' response to them was, "If you had faith (trust and confidence in God) even as a grain of mustard seed, you could say to this mulberry tree, Be pulled up by the roots, and be planted in the sea, and it would obey you."

Often we look at human suffering, become overwhelmed and decide that we just do not have enough faith to pray about it. Jesus wants us to use the faith that we already have and begin to ask Him for healing. That is what I did during a crisis in our family and the answer astounded me.

After my father's death, which was followed by serious financial setbacks, my mother began to suffer from severe clinical depression. Often suicidal, she would call and threaten to kill herself if I could not drive the sixty miles to visit her. Being the mother of two little boys, I could not always be available. When I could not go, the bitterness in her soul poured over me in a scalding verbal assault. If you have ever been in a situation like this, you know that tormented people often torment those who care for them.

For the next six years, I was my mother's primary caretaker. As her depression deepened, the kind, fun-loving person I had known as "Mother" slowly disappeared. We sought the help of many physicians and she went through many hospitalizations. Finally, all human effort had run out. Her last physician suggested that I commit her to the state hospital for the mentally ill where she would probably stay until she died.

Before I would agree to his suggestion, I visited with Mother once more. As usual, she was in "lock-up," living in a room with bars on the windows. She wore a faded, gray hospital gown. As I entered her room, I found her looking out of the window at the sunlight that shown through the bright golden leaves of a large maple tree. She turned from the window and asked, "Is it daytime or nighttime?" I shall never forget the terror I felt when I realized that Mother could no longer perceive light. She had become one of the living dead. It was over. I agreed to return in a week and make arrangements for her transfer.

At that point, God sent a new friend into my life who believed in the power of prayer. Even though I had "grown up" in church, I had never heard of a single person who had received an answer to prayer. I had not encountered faith. Because of my new friend's influence, I sincerely asked God for help for the first time in my life.

My prayer was not very spiritual and I had little faith. I asked, "Lord, if You know where I am right now and if You know that my mother has been sick for years, please heal her. I simply cannot continue to take her from one hospital to another. If you can't make her well and keep her well, just help me get her to a safe place. Amen."

A week later, I returned to the hospital. As I met with her physician, he folded his hands, leaned across his desk, looked me right in the eye and said, "Lynda, I cannot explain this to you. All I know is that your mother has come to herself. Actually, she appears to be well. She deserves a chance to go home and begin to live again."

I simply could not believe him! How could this have happened? Was it really an answer to prayer? Suddenly, nothing seemed quite real. In response to my questions, he replied, "I wish that I could take credit for the change in your mother, but I cannot. All I know is that when I walked into her room one morning this week, she was a different person."

At his suggestion, in a startled daze, I went to visit Mother. She was no longer in lock-up. I found her in the recreation room having coffee with several other women. The first thing I noticed was that she was wearing her own clothes again. The hospital gown had been discarded. When she saw me, I was amazed by the light in her eyes. There was almost a twinkle there. Her first words were, "Oh, honey, can you ever forgive me for all I've done to you?"

I cannot describe the various emotions that ran through my mind . . . joy, disbelief, fear of the future, anticipation of the future and more joy. I had encountered the healing power of God. I had actually contacted Jesus through prayer and He had healed my mother. Through a request made, with just a little faith, a remarkable answer had been given.

Our next year was filled with transition, forgiveness and healing. Because there was so little biblical training available to her, plus a lack of opportunity for continued counseling, Mother did not grow to her full potential for happiness. However, she returned to her home and was able to live alone there as an independent woman until she was 88 years old.

The Word of God

Hebrews 4:12 tells us that the Word that God speaks is "alive and full of power—making it active, operative, energizing and effective." When we put God's Word into our minds, a spiritual transaction takes place that affects our entire beings. There is power in the Word.

Proverbs 6:20–22 tells us: "Keep your father's [God-given] commandment, and forsake not the law of [God] your mother [taught you]. Bind them continually upon your heart. . . . When you go, [the Word of your parents' God] it shall lead you; when you sleep, it shall keep you, and when you waken, it shall talk with you."

When I was sick, I decided to take those words literally. I looked up all of the Scriptures I could find that referred to health and healing and recorded them on tape. I taped my own voice agreeing with God's Word, receiving His promises. I asked God to cause the Holy Spirit to imprint the unshakable truth of His Word in my mind. When I went to bed at night, I inserted my earphones and played the tape all through the night. When I awoke the next morning, even though I had usually turned the tape off sometime during the night, my first thoughts would be those that my mind had absorbed from the Word. I believe that His powerful Word continually rescued and guarded my mind from depression and discouragement, enabling me to continue my healing search.

A friend named Dave told me how God's Word brought about a healing change in his heart and mind. He said, "I am amazed at how we settle for the pain in our lives when God has a clear solution for so much of it. When I was growing up, my parents were good providers in many ways, but we did not connect emotionally. We were distant from each other. When I became an adult, I had no idea what intimacy was, and I became an 'emotional taker.' God was gracious to give me a wife who was loyal and steadfast, but she was needy also. We were both 'stuffers' of our emotions. There were things I wanted to tell her, but my insecurities ran so deep that I feared the consequences. I thought I would surely lose her."

Dave told me about the profound effect of God's Word. "My wife and I finally decided to attend a marriage seminar. When the leader announced that we were going to 'experience the Scripture' during our time together, I had no idea what he meant. He offered us James 5:16, asking us to confess our faults one to another. Even though I was still afraid, I decided to obey God's Word and related several hidden memories and feelings to my wife. Until that moment, I don't believe I had ever felt that I was loved unconditionally by another person. As I humbled myself in faith, I felt a great outpouring of my wife's love.

"When God exposed my loneliness and neediness, I did not feel alone. I began to experience Genesis 2:18— that it is not good for man to be alone. My wife and I wept with each other over our missed relationships at home, over the hurt of unmet needs of our children and the sinful ways in which we had attempted to meet our own needs. Then, we chose to experience Ephesians 4:31–32 by forgiving those who had hurt us . . . and we were free to make a new start.

"After that point, I felt God's love at a level I had never dreamed of. Since the emotional poisons of fear, guilt and shame had been emptied from my life, other benefits have also come. I no longer go to food for comfort, so my weight is in a healthy range. Several severe stomach symptoms have disappeared and my energy level is great. I am generally healthier and more disease-resistant. Not only that, but I am happy, positive and more filled with God's Spirit than ever before."

Dave's story fully illustrates the power of God's Word to heal and deliver. Whatever your condition is, I suggest that you research God's Word and apply it to your mind and heart as a medicine. If you store God's Word in your mind, then even if you are in such a desperate emotional state that you cannot read or think, the Holy Spirit will bring God's Word back to you.

For example, Maribeth told me about a time when she was so distraught and depressed that she could not pray. "A chain of events left me in total despair," she said. "I found myself lying on the floor of our country home listening to the sound of the freight train as it passed by. I felt the dark pull of temptation to end my life. The thought persisted, *Just go out and lie down on the tracks and the pain will soon be over.* That thought battered my mind all night long. Then a mental picture came into my mind of Jesus on the cross and His Word from Hebrews 13 followed: 'Never will I leave you. Never will I forsake you.'

"As the night went on, the power of the Word was the only thing that caused me to cling to my life. It held me steady. That night was my turning point. A few days later I went into counseling and began to face my hurt and fears, forgiving all who had harmed me. Over a period of months, the overwhelming grief of my losses began slowly to fade and be replaced with faith for the future. I had hope again. The Word had come and it had delivered me" (see Psalm 107:20).

It is important to know God's Word *before* we find ourselves in a crisis, so that we may recall it under pressure.

Recently I met Brother White, a pastor who told me how God's Word sustained him through a severe heart attack.

"My wife and I stopped at a fast food restaurant and were driving through to pick up our food when the pain started. It began in my jaw, went to my throat and then passed into my chest. Three years ago, I had suffered from severe heart problems and had been healed through surgery, so I was familiar with that kind of pain. I realized that my car was parked so close to the building that no one could open my door and get me out of the car. As the pain intensified, I made efforts to move my car away from the building, repeating the name of Jesus over and over. As soon as I got my car to a safe place, I passed out. My wife asked someone to call an ambulance and I was transported to the nearest hospital. My wife prayed constantly, 'Father, just don't let there be any damage.'"

Tests were run over a period of hours, but Brother White's heart stabilized and he was sent home the next day.

Three weeks later, the pains began again. Brother White explained: "I knew that I was in major trouble, so we went to the Baptist Hospital in Little Rock. Tests were run and that day and night I was given morphine for the pain. In spite of the medication, my pain was still severe. I was tempted to let myself sink into fear, but I decided to reject fear and believe God's Word." Brother White repeated to himself over and over one of his favorite Scripture passages, Isaiah 43:1–2:

> Fear not, for I have redeemed you—ransomed you by paying a price instead of leaving you captives; I have called you by your name, you are Mine. When you pass through the waters I will be with you, and through the rivers they shall not overwhelm you; when you walk through the fire you shall not be burned or scorched, nor shall the flame kindle upon you.

Brother White continued, "You see, you cannot fight this kind of battle with a big stick or a gun. You cannot fight something you cannot see. You have to use God's Word as your weapon. I knew that I was in deep waters. I could not touch bottom. God's Word was my weapon and my solid ground. Even though the nurses gave morphine, the pain continued all through the night. I continued to repeat God's Word to myself."

The pain ceased by morning and more tests were begun. When the cardiologist returned with the results, he said, "I can't find anything wrong with your heart, Brother White. In fact, I can't even find scar tissue from your last surgery." Brother White was given a clean bill of health and released from the hospital. He began preaching again the next day and has been healthy ever since.

Medical Science

Have you ever thought about the number of medications, procedures and technologies made available to us during the last century? Some of these advances include antibiotics, the Salk vaccine, MRIs, lasers, chemotherapy, laparoscopy, angiography, gene splicing, blood tests for detecting diseases such as cancer and HIV, nuclear medicine scans, heart valves, organ transplants, microsurgery, psychotropic medications for depression and anxiety, estrogen therapy, birth control, kidney dialysis, implants for hearing, pacemakers, and artificial knee and hip joints. Computers have fast-forwarded medical discoveries during the last ten years. Almost every day there are announcements about new cures. We have been truly blessed.

When "scientific methods" are used to heal people, we often tend to diminish God's participation. We need to remember that all knowledge comes from God, as well as the wisdom and creativity needed to combine areas of knowledge into effective treatment. Every substance that is used in medications and technology was given to us by God. We see evidence of man being granted the grace to break new frontiers in medical science every day.

We need to view medical science as a gift from God. If He chooses to use the knowledge and equipment of medical science to cure us, it does not mean that His concern is not just as great or that we have received inferior grace. God's grace toward us is full and perfect. His methods of healing us are personal and effective, treating the whole person.

John, a successful businessman, attests to this: "I had bypass surgery last year. Even with all of the new techniques, I could hardly believe the brevity of my recovery time. I've learned a great deal about diet and exercise, and with the availability of health information over the Internet, I feel that I have been able to learn what I need to know to remain healthy. I thank God for modern technology: He used it to save my life and protect my future health. In fact, I had been a workaholic since my college years, taking my health for granted. I needed that hard dose of reality. I needed time to think and change my priorities, to learn to slow down. This has been the best year of my life." God not only granted healing to John's heart, but He gave him an opportunity to reflect and change his way of living.

Miracles

First Corinthians 12:10 tells us that the Body of Christ has been granted gifts of miracles. Perhaps the reason that we do not witness more miracles today is that we simply do not believe. Even when Jesus was on the earth, He was not able to do miracles at certain places because of the unbelief of the people there (see Matthew 13:58). Since God's Word tells us specifically that gifts of miracles are available, it could be a fatal oversight on our part to ignore this possibility.

My friend Carolyn told me of a small boy who would probably not be alive today if the people praying for him had not had the faith to pray for a miracle. It happened almost thirty years ago. "Rose, a Latin American Catholic woman, had been working in our home for two years," Carolyn said. "She began to voice her concerns for her five-year-old son, Jamie. She told me that he was having dizzy spells, bumping into things and that his speech was sometimes incoherent. The doctors at St. Joseph's Hospital found the evidence of more than one tumor on Jamie's brain.

"Brain surgery was scheduled. I went to the hospital to be with Rose. To my surprise, Rose welcomed me, saying, 'Mrs. J., Jamie told me that Jesus came to him and told him that everything was going to be all right and not to worry.' I was astounded and almost afraid to hope.

"I returned to the waiting room and found Betty, Rose's sister, and other family members. I told Betty that Rose and I had laid hands on Jamie for one final prayer for healing. Betty replied, 'You don't really believe God is going to heal him, do you?' I felt bombarded by doubt and fear. Somehow I managed to respond, 'Yes, I really do believe God will heal him.' At that point we all prayed for Jamie once more.

"Just moments later Rose and her husband joined us, and Rose began to tell us of the plans she had for Jamie when he recovered. 'I think I'll have him repeat kindergarten, because he's missed so much school,' she stated. I was in awe of this mother's faith.

"When several minutes had passed, a message came over the loud speaker, requesting that Jamie's parents come to the surgical floor immediately. They flew down the hall, and when they returned their jubilant smiles lit up the corridor. Rose exclaimed, 'The doctors took one more x-ray and there was absolutely no trace of any tumors! The doctors are baffled and want to do some more tests before they think about surgery.'

"Jamie stayed at St. Joe's for three more days. He had no dizziness, his coordination was good and his speech was normal. All the tests were negative. The doctors puzzled over the two sets of x-rays, one revealing tumors and one showing a healthy brain. Finally they sent Jamie home, declaring a miracle of God."

Carolyn concluded Jamie's story, "Now, back to the prayers we had prayed. One was that Jesus would reveal Himself to Jamie. Another was that Rose would come to know Christ more closely. After Jamie was healed, Rose said, 'I feel as though I have been born again.' Another was the gift of faith, which God gave me when Betty questioned God's desire to heal Jamie. The gift of faith was also displayed as Rose planned for Jamie's future."

Do you think Jamie's miracle would have occurred without the prayer of faith? What would have happened if the women had not known and believed that God would perform a miraculous healing today? We need to know what God says He will do and call upon Him to do it. James tells us that we have not because we ask not. All of the women who prayed for Jamie and his family were new Christians. However, they knew God's Word, believed it and had the faith to apply it.

A woman named Deb from Wisconsin told of a miracle in her life. "I was chaperoning a youth trip last summer when I began to have seizures. The first episode occurred at the end of a worship service when I began having violent muscle spasms that lasted forty-five minutes. Following that, I had multiple episodes, five to eight seizures per hour. Some were mild head jerking while others threw me to the floor for long, exhausting events.

"At first medications controlled the spasms, but in a month the medicine had lost its effectiveness. New medication with bad side effects replaced the milder medication, but it did help to limit the number of episodes. By fall the spasms were increasing in severity and after two emergency trips to the hospital, the doctor prescribed bottles of oxygen in my house to help me breathe during the spasms.

"In October, we called for the elders of the church to come and pray for me. Before they arrived, I wrote a list of my needs and requests. I listed the following petitions:

1. I do not want to fall on the floor any more.
2. I want to be able to breathe freely.
3. I do not want my head to jerk any more.
4. I want my arms, hands and feet to stop jerking.
5. I want my eyes not to roll back so that I cannot see.
6. I want no more repetitive medical tests.
7. I really desire a non-medical answer.
8. I want a finite time of medication followed by normal living.
9. I never want to lose the lesson of compassion I have received from this experience.

10. I want my life back, but with all the lessons I have learned intact and ingrained.

"After the elders prayed, one by one my prayers were answered. First the falling on the floor and then another and another. The answers came so gradually over the next month that they were almost imperceptible. The elders actually thought my medicine was working better and that the dosage was regulated correctly.

"Since early fall, my doctor had been trying to get me into the Mayo Clinic. In November I got into the clinic and was required to leave off all medications for twenty-four hours before arriving for treatment. During that twenty-four hours, I had no symptoms. When the doctors at Mayo Clinic completed their examination of me, they said that I had no sign of any disease and could return home to a normal life.

"The Body of Christ on its knees can move mountains. How I thank Him for this wonderful act of mercy! It has been almost six months since I returned from the Mayo Clinic and all is well."

As Deb said, "The Body of Christ on its knees can move mountains." We have a merciful, faithful God and we should not hesitate to ask for or expect a miracle when we make our requests of Him. Even if there are times when there is no evidence that He is working, remain faithful in prayer. Listen carefully for His instructions and wait.

Laughter

Much research has been done recently on the healing effects of laughter. Proverbs 17:22, in the King James Version, tells us that "a merry heart doeth good like a medicine." Now, centuries later, science has confirmed the words of King Solomon.

Jane, a nurse, explained the physiological and psychological effects of laughter to me. She said, "Scientists have found that laughter is a form of internal 'jogging' that exercises internal organs and stimulates the release of beneficial neurotransmitters and hormones."

Then she pointed out, "You know, children laugh hundreds of times a day, but adults don't laugh nearly as much. If we will learn to laugh again more easily and often, it would have a positive effect on our overall well-being. Laughter is one of the body's safety valves, a counterbalance to tension. Because we live such fast-paced, stress-filled lives, our level of stress hormones can become overloaded. When we laugh, the elevated levels of the body's stress hormones drop back to normal. When our bodies stay in a healthy balance, our immune systems can stay strong. A number of facilities around the country are establishing laughter clinics in order to give patients a healthy edge for recovery."

A little humor can provide comic relief at stressful times. When I was going to the hospital for spine surgery to have a broken disk removed, our older son, David, called and asked, "Now, Mom, are you going to be even shorter after surgery?" This was a humorous moment for our family because I am only five feet two inches tall, and my husband and sons are over six feet. As our sons were growing up and their height outdistanced mine, they would tease me about my right to "tell them what to do" because I was so short. I laughed about this with the nurse while she was preparing me for surgery, and our laughter helped alleviate some of the last-minute anxiety.

Natural Foods and Herbs

Many of us know little about the healing effects of natural foods and herbs. However, discoveries in this area are breaking new ground every day. Numerous articles indicate that the proper food can make the difference between life and death. Some relate how food can fight everything from fat to cancer, and some recommend herbs to cure sinus problems, stomach aches, headaches and urinary tract problems. The use of vitamins and supplements has been known to cure disease.

A woman named Carlen, who doubted the validity of natural substances, became willing to experiment after struggling with multiple sclerosis for five years. The rewards of her willingness were apparent as she stated: "I was 34 years old when I was diagnosed with multiple sclerosis. My husband and I were directors at Teen Challenge, so my need for energy and health was vital.

"In my fifth year of this disease, I felt that God was telling me that diet was one of the elements He wanted to use in my life to bring restoration. As I pondered that possibility, my condition grew worse. I had the type of MS that gets worse without remission. Every year since my initial diagnosis, my symptoms had increased. I could stand or walk for only about five minutes before having to lie down. My vision was blurry. I had frequent headaches, ringing in my ears, poor concentration, inability to sleep and extreme fatigue. My digestion and bladder were affected. I used a wheelchair when I left my house.

"We were at a critical point in the ministry. It had become impossible for us to continue in such demanding positions unless my condition improved. One day a friend called and recommended a specific brand of supplements. She said that those substances, along with a healthy diet, had caused enormous improvements in her health. I began to study the subject and read testimonies of nutritionists and nurses. I was still reluctant to believe that a different diet and supplements could relieve such a serious illness as MS.

"One night I awoke and felt the presence of the Holy Spirit. At that time, I became convinced that I should start the use of the supplements. With little real faith in the program, I began. Within a month, I was following an exercise video two times a week. This gradually increased to five times a week. My sleep patterns became normal. Within six months, I was able to ride a bike for fifteen or twenty minutes. I could swim. I could walk on the beach. I went kayaking! I was putting in a twelve-hour workday. I had no fatigue problems.

"Where muscles had atrophied, I was visibly seeing muscle mass growing after only about two months of exercise. It is so exciting. I was given a new life! My husband was given a new wife! It has been a year and two months since I began the diet, supplements and exercise. In my life, *MS* no longer stands for 'multiple sclerosis' but for the 'Master's Salvation.'"

If you are suffering from an emotional or physical illness, it would be wise to gain knowledge in the area of complementary and alternative medications and foods. God has filled the earth with healing.

Our Highest Purpose

God's healing power is being poured out upon His children today. His Word shows us how to remove any blocks that may keep us from receiving from Him. By His strength He helps us endure as we seek His healing touch. He has placed many avenues of healing in the earth. He wants us to receive. Our eternal purpose, however, is not to receive healing, but to know Him. As Paul said, "[For my determined purpose is] that I may know Him—that I may progressively become more deeply and intimately acquainted with Him, perceiving and recognizing and understanding [the wonders of His Person] more strongly and more clearly" (Philippians 3:10).

It is my belief that the best is always ahead for a believer—even beyond life on the earth, for there is a greater life ahead that will never end. The future of every believer is glorious. Revelation 21:4 tells us that "God will wipe away every tear from their eyes, and death shall be no more, neither shall there be anguish—sorrow and mourning—nor grief nor pain any more; for the old conditions and the former order of things have passed away."

At some point, every type of pain will cease forever. There is a cut-off point! Until then, let us turn confidently to Jehovah Rapha our Healer, Jesus our Savior and the Holy Spirit who is God on the earth today. Our God is always on our side.

My prayer for you comes from 3 John 2: "Beloved, I pray that you may prosper in every way and [that your body] may keep well, even as [I know] your soul keeps well and prospers."

Suggested Prayer

Jehovah Rapha, Lord Jesus Christ and Holy Spirit, You have offered healing and wholeness to me in so many ways. Your ways are varied and they are many. Your power and mercy are great. Your love and provisions for us never end. They become more and more glorious. The peace You give is everlasting. No foe can defeat You. I am safe in Your care. You are my Helper and my Teacher. You are my Redeemer and my Burden-Bearer. Your lovingkindness never fails me. You, Jesus, are my hope and my expectation.

How can I give You glory? Lord, take all that I am and let me reflect who You are. Live in me, Holy Spirit, and let me be a reflection of Your healing work. O Lord, You are my God.

"Heal me, O Lord, and I shall be healed; save me, and I shall be saved; for You are my praise" (Jeremiah 17:14). Amen.

Dear Readers,

When I was nine years old, I wrote a story. My mother typed it, made a cover with my name on it and announced that someday I would probably write a real book. As I proudly showed the little booklet to my father, I never dreamed that the illnesses my parents suffered would lead to my writing a book about healing.

God wastes absolutely nothing that happens to us in life. He will even use past suffering to bring about future healing. It is my joy to tell you now what we did not know when my parents were suffering physically and emotionally.

It is my heart's desire to help you receive God's love and truth, hope and healing.

Lynda Elliott

Lynda Elliott is a licensed social worker who offers counseling to individuals and families. In addition to *An Invitation to Healing,* she has written *The Counsel of a Friend,* and co-authored *My Father's Child: Help and Healing for Victims of Childhood Physical, Emotional, and Sexual Abuse.*

Lynda is an adjunct faculty member of Trinity College and Seminary, providing courses for women internationally, and she enjoys teaching at conferences and seminars. Some of her topics include God's Avenues for Healing; Healing from Depression; Removing Blocks to Healing; Healing from Childhood Abuse: Help for Parents of Grown-Up Children; How to Help One Another (Lay Counseling for the Church); and What Is Forgiveness?

Lynda and her husband, Wayne, live in Little Rock, Arkansas, and have two grown sons and four grand-children.

If you are interested in having Lynda Elliott speak at a conference or workshop, you may reach her by calling (501) 224-5015 or e-mailing her at:
<L-WElliott@juno.com>